INSIGHT COMPACT GUIDES

Lake District

Compact Guide: Lake District is the ideal reference guide to this perennially popular English region. It tells you all you need to know about making the most of its attractions, from Druids' circles to wildlife parks, from the Wordsworth Museum to Beatrix Potter's House.

This is one of more than 70 titles in *Apa Publications'* new series of pocket-sized, easy-to-use guidebooks intended for the independent-minded traveller. *Compact Guides* are in essence travel encyclopedias in miniature, designed to be comprehensive yet portable, as well as up-to-date and authoritative.

Star Attractions

An instant reference to some of the Lake District's top attractions to help you establish your priorities.

Sizergh Castle p15

Windermere Steamboat Museum p19

Aira Force p23

Hartsop p24

Townend House, Troutbeck p25

Tarn Hows p29

Dove Cottage p37

Lakeland Sheep and Wool Centre p47

Beatrix Potter's House p63

Cartmel Priory p59

Grizedale Forest p59

Lake DISTRICT

Introduction

Places

Culture

Leisure

Practical Information

Lake District – Splendour on a Small Scale

Opposite: moody view of the Langdales

For a million years, the Lake District was the playground of glaciers. A mass of ice bit deeply into an ancient landscape, plucking, gouging and smoothing to create the characteristic deep lakes and steep-sided valleys. But it isn't just the forces of nature that have conspired to make the Lake District the most striking landscape in England. Dramatic details have been added on, such as the white-washed farms on rock ledges and white-faced Herdwicks, Lakeland's own little sheep, their eyes looking as ancient as the rocks among which they forage for their herby diet. Wild daffodils flourish in the deciduous woods and also near the shore of Ullswater, where they were seen by William Wordsworth. His poem about 'dancing daffodils' which begins 'I wandered lonely as a cloud', is one of the best-known in the English language.

An energetic person could walk across the Lake District, from Ennerdale in the west to Shap in the east, in 24 hours – a distance of about 40 miles (65km) as the crow flies. In the European context, the Lake District is tiny, yet here is a region of infinite variety. Shaped like a giant wheel, its ridges radiate from a hub of high mountains (known by the Norse term of 'fells'), enfolding a host of little valleys called 'dales' and a score of big lakes. The landscape is on a comprehensible scale, not spread out as in the Scottish Highlands where mountains stand aloof from the glens and the lochs seem to go on forever. From Great End, near the heart of the district, the view north extends over Solway Firth to the blue hills of Scotland and, eastwards, to the Howgill Fells, beyond Lunesdale. The distant blue-grey smudge is the Pennines. To the west and south the sun brings a responsible gleam from the sea.

At the summit

5

Seen from a distance, the fells appear to spring from low country – from the Cumbrian Plain in the north, the fan-shaped Eden Valley in the east and the coastal strip of the west. Viewed from the south, the fells loom beyond a fringe of pearl-white limestone. On clear days, strollers on the 'prom' at Morecambe who look across the Bay have a clear view of Black Combe, a giant brooding in isolation in the southwest of the Lake District.

By the lake shore

On a Bank Holiday, over a quarter of a million day-trippers invade the Lake District from the conurbations of the Northeast, Yorkshire and Lancashire. Yet a short stroll away from the crowds leads to peaceful areas. Even Orrest Head, the modest knoll above Windermere, long celebrated as a vantage point, is not likely to be crowded. Half a century ago, this eminence inspired the young Alfred Wainwright (1906–91) to leave his native Lancashire textile town for Kendal, where he began his little hand-written guides to the Lakeland Fells.

Location and size

The Lake District is a tourist's name for the heart of Cumbria. Before local government boundaries changed in 1974, the region was divided between Cumberland, Westmorland, northern Lancashire and the West Riding of Yorkshire. The Lake District National Park covers an area of 880 sq miles (2,279 sq km). This northwest corner of England is virtually an island, being washed by salt water on three sides and having an asphalt 'moat', consisting of six lanes of the M6, in the east.

The local term for lake is 'watter' or 'mere' – hence Wastwater and Windermere. Only one stretch of water has 'lake' in its title, and that is Bassenthwaite Lake, to the north of Keswick.

Geology

The geology of the area is complex. The most perceptive early student of the rocks was Jonathan Otley, of Keswick, who in 1820 published an article about 'the succession of rocks in the District of the Lakes', identifying three basic types. Knowing these simplifies the subject for the layman. Skiddaw slates, the oldest visible rocks, form the friable northern fells plus that isolated bulk of Black Combe in the southwest. They were laid down over 500 million years ago in a shallow sea. Some 50 million years later, a volcano flared. The Borrowdale volcanics of Central Lakeland were born of flame, smoke and lava-flows in a drama of landscape-formation which lasted about a million years. The Silurian slates of the Southern Lakes, composed of shales, slates, grits and flags, are (like the Skiddaw group) sedimentary. A fourth major geological element forms a narrow band of Coniston limestone between the volcanics and the Silurian slates. Clear evidence of it is to be seen by anyone who travels between the village of Coniston and Ambleside.

The appearance of the Lake District was determined 50–60 million years ago, a great period of mountain building which also thrust up the Alps and the Himalayas. In Cumbria, an immense dome was created. The radial drainage cut into the dome. During the Ice Age, ice sculpted the fells, created 'hanging' valleys, deepened and smoothed the old river valleys. The climate ameliorated and the glaciers melted some 10,000 years ago.

When first gouged out by ice, the lakes had affinities with one another. They have since changed at varying rates, depending on their situation and the way in which the adjacent land has been used. The least changed lake is Wastwater, in the far west, whose blueish tinge hints at near-sterility. By contrast, centuries of human settlement and intensive farming around the shallow, reed-edged

6

The Old Mill at Ambleside

Ice-Age boulders at Kentmere

Esthwaite Water, by Hawkshead, have enriched the water. Windermere, the largest lake, is more than 10 miles (16km) long but relatively narrow. Ullswater, which comes second in size, is unlike the other lakes in that it has two bends. Its head is among the high fells, its tail in the pleasant pastoral landscape around Pooley Bridge. In addition to the big lakes, there are mountain tarns, which the artist W. Heaton Cooper called 'the eyes of the mountains'.

On Carrock Fell

7

Climate

Lakeland's climate is affected by the proximity of the sea and by the high fells, which form a barrier to weatherfronts sweeping in from the west. The western fells are a great cloud-factory, coaxing the prevailing wind to part with its moisture. Seathwaite, in Borrowdale, tucked away among high fells near the centre of the area, has long been famous as the wettest inhabited spot in England, the rainfall being about 125 inches (3,175mm) a year.

Seathwaite's reputation for wetness was established when, in 1844, the manager of the graphite mine agreed to a request by a student of water supplies to take regular readings of the rainfall and the first year's total was an astonishing 152 inches (3,860mm). Little has changed: in August 1966, for example, 4–5 inches (100–130mm) descended on the Seathwaite area in a little over an hour, causing serious flooding and damage to property.

On dull days there are usually breaks in the cloud through which sunlight streams with all the intensity of a spotlight at the theatre, bringing sections of the landscape into sharp relief. When Lakeland has a bonnet of cloud, sunlight puts a gleam on Morecambe Bay or St Bees Head. There is no permanent snow cover, but pockets may linger in deep gullies until midsummer. With most of the major valleys at low elevation, a dale might remain green when the flanking fells are gleaming white with snow.

A break in the cloud

Farming stock

A pastoral landscape

Five thousand years have elapsed since humankind made its first mark on the Lake District landscape, clearing away tracts of the old forest that extended up the hills as far as the 2,000-ft (600-m) contour. A thousand years ago, Norse settlers adjusted their lifestyle to the high hills, on which they summered their cattle and sheep. From such a hardy, independent, self-reliant stock has evolved a type of farming which has its equivalent systems in mountainous areas all over the world.

When Norman lords granted the monastic orders large tracts of the Lake District, these became a range for sheep bred from the native 'crag' sheep. They became known as Herdwicks, after monastic pastures, and the name is used to this day for the nimble little animal which has a face white as hoar-frost, a coarse fleece which is dark at first, becoming greyer with age, and four solid legs to enable it to cope with the mountainous grazing.

Farming is the basic industry of Lakeland and the one of which a visitor is most aware. The farms have stocks of sheep and a few beef cattle. Tending the sheep gives plenty of work for well-trained curs or collies, which respond to the whistles of the farmer with barks (vital here when flushing sheep from among rocks or dense areas of bracken). The Lakeland farmer is just as spirited as his forebears, who were greatly admired by William Wordsworth and his friends.

Local breeds

Mining and tourism

The dalehead farmhouses, many of which date from the 17th century, were built of stone and slate (*see page 62*). Evidence of slate quarrying is to be found in many places. In the quest for good slate, quarrymen became miners. It is exciting to enter an old quarry, with pieces of slate clinking underfoot, and stand at the entrance of a man-made cave (on no account explore underground workings). In some cases, the extent of the underground works can be deduced from the draught of warm air on the face. Slate is still quarried at the Burlington Quarry south of Coniston, at Elterwater and near the Kirkstone Pass.

From Lake District fells have come a variety of minerals, including copper, which was mined in various places, notably the Newlands Valley. Graphite, also known as 'wadd', was hewn from underground workings near Seathwaite, at the head of Borrowdale, and became the origin of the Keswick pencil industry. Granite of various hues is quarried at Shap. The exploitation of iron ore in Eskdale led to the building of the 3-ft (0.9-m) gauge railway in 1875. In the following year, that line passed to public use. It endures today as a tourist line – the Ravenglass & Eskdale Railway (affectionately known as Ratty).

Tourism is paramount in the Lakeland economy. In fact, the whole area is fast becoming a theme park. The work of Beatrix Potter, creator of the immortal Peter Rabbit, Jemima Puddleduck and friends, has given rise to shops dealing exclusively with her books and associated souvenirs. The National Trust, the largest landowner in the Lake District, owns Hill Top, her property at Near Sawrey, and the diminutive building at nearby Hawkshead, where her husband, William Heelis, had his solicitor's office.

Wildlife

The red deer is well represented in the wooded valleys of Grizedale Forest and on Claife Heights, to the west of Windermere. Red deer also occur at Thirlmere and Martindale, the last-named being a secluded valley beyond Howtown (Ullswater). Roe deer are widespread again, though deer-fencing around new plantations inhibits their movement in some areas.

The red fox is common, despite the activities of six foxhound packs, and badgers are found mainly in the old deciduous woods. Otters are now scarce in the Lake District proper – the best chance of seeing them is to join an otter-watching party organised at the bird reserve of Leighton Moss, near Silverdale, just outside the southern boundary of Cumbria. For years, the Lake District has been a stronghold of the red squirrel. It is still well represented in old woodland, but now the larger, more vigorous grey squirrel has gained access and is slowly extending its bounds at the expense of the smaller, daintier red. The grey has appeared as far north as Grasmere.

9

Sculpture and rhododendrons in Grizedale Forest

The Lake District is famous for its cliff-nesting species, notably the pair of golden eagles that for years have nested on a crag above Rigginedale near Haweswater and may be observed from a RSPB hide in that dale. Peregrine falcons, ravens and buzzards, which nest in fell country, are relatively common. The pied flycatcher is well suited to the mature woods. This summer visitor also takes readily to nest boxes, which has given it a wider distribution than previously. Canada geese are frequently seen around Grasmere, and greylag geese are locally common by Derwent Water and Coniston Water.

Of fish, the once-migratory char became land-locked towards the end of the Ice Age but still frequents deep water in some of the lakes, notably Windermere. Expert anglers operate from rowing boats, each man with one or more long rods, with groups of hooks extending from a main line which, having been weighted, goes to a depth of up to 90ft (27m). Of the other locally distributed fish, the schelly (a sort of freshwater herring) is associated with Ullswater. A white fish called the vendace is found in Bassenthwaite and Derwent Water.

Historical Highlights

4500BC The first hunter-fishermen appear in the Lake District.

3500BC A thriving Neolithic culture develops. Much clearing of the native forest. Cultivation of crops and keeping of livestock.

around 2500BC The first Lakeland industry is the production of axeheads from a durable and knappable volcanic tuff found high on Stickle Pike (Great Langdale) and on Scafell Pike.

around 1400BC A stone circle is set on a hill now known as Castlerigg, east of Keswick. It may have been the focal point for a local tribe.

1st century AD Roman domination of the fell country is maintained by a system of roads driven through the terrain of a Celtic people known as the Brigantes.

383 Hadrian's Wall abandoned. Roman rule in the northwest crumbles with the withdrawal of troops. Local Celts, isolated by incursions of Anglo-Saxons from the east, become known as the Cymry (hence the county name 'Cumberland').

7th century People of Anglian farming stock from Northumbria arrive in the peripheral areas of the Lake District and begin to work the most fertile ground. They leave a lasting memorial in finely-carved stone crosses. St Herbert, friend of Cuthbert, is to be found at a hermitage on an island in Derwentwater.

9th–10th centuries Norse-Irish settlement from the west proves to be the last great immigration. The newcomers, also known as Vikings (from *vik*, meaning creek) follow a tradition well established in their ancestral Norway – of farms in the valleys, which they call dales, and *saeters* or summer grazings on the mountainsides, which they call fells.

1092 Following the Norman Conquest, William II takes Carlisle from the Scottish king and settles the area with people brought from the south. The Norman lords make grants to monastic orders, who from abbeys at the periphery of the Lake District maintained their properties in the dale through 'granges'.

1322 Robert the Bruce, at the head of a Scottish raiding force, visits Furness and uses the Oversands Route to attack Lancaster. A defence against repetitive Scottish raids is the pele tower, stoutly built of stone and provisioned, becoming a safe retreat for local people and their stock.

1454 First mention of a ferry across Windermere, from a point south of Bowness, in Westmorland, to the Lancashire shore.

1564 The Company of Mines Royal (a Crown monopoly) prospects for minerals (copper, lead and silver) in the Keswick area. Expert guidance is given by about 50 mining experts brought in from Germany. Mining takes place in the Newlands Valley and on Coniston Old Man.

1618 George Preston of Holker Hall, with local help, repairs Cartmel Priory. Since the Dissolution, only the nave of this striking building had been used, the rest of the building being stripped of its roof for the value of the lead.

1626 George Browne, a yeoman farmer, builds Townend, in the village of Troutbeck.

1640–1750 Timber-framed buildings, roofed with thatch, are replaced by stone houses and farms. In many cases, the proud owners have the date and their initials carved on the lintel.

1643 Slate quarries are opened beside Honister Pass. Quarrymen's cottages are built at Seatoller, in Borrowdale.

1650 Ambleside is granted its charter as a market town.

1680 The Hasell family becomes associated with Dalemain, near Ullswater, and subsequently their grand house, at the core of which is a 12th-century pele tower, is fronted by pink sandstone.

1718 Lowther Village, on the vast estate of the Earls of Lonsdale near Penrith, is created as a model village for estate workers. The scheme is designed by the Adam brothers.

1750–1850 Enclosure period creates a new landscape of fields and dry-stone walls.

1799 William Wordsworth and his sister Dorothy take up residence at what is now known as Dove Cottage, Grasmere.

1813 Construction of the Moot Hall on an island site at Keswick. Wordsworth and his family take up residence at Rydal Hall. He becomes Distributor of Stamps for Westmorland and has his office in Ambleside.

1835 Harriet Martineau, writer and social reformer, moves into The Knoll at Ambleside. She will live there until her death in 1876.

1852 The first recorded Grasmere Sports meeting is held.

1845 The first steam yacht, named *Lady of the Lake*, goes into service on Lake Windermere.

1847 The railway reaches Birthwaite, which soon blossoms into a town named Windermere. Tourism flourishes. Rigg's Windermere Hotel sets a new standard for size and quality.

1854 Internment at Caldbeck of the huntsman John Peel (born at Park End, Caldbeck, 1776). The words of the song *D'ye Ken John Peel?* carry on his memory.

1859 The Furness Railway is extended to Coniston. Subsequently, the company introduces a steamer service to Coniston Water with the *Gondola*. On Ullswater, a steamer service is inaugurated, from Glenridding to Pooley Bridge.

1864 Life at Keswick is transformed with the coming of the railway from Penrith.

1869 A railway opens from Plumpton, near Ulverston, to Lakeside. The Furness Railway introduces 'screw' steamers to Lake Windermere, the first being the *Swan*.

1872 John Ruskin – writer, artist and philosopher – acquires Brantwood, on the east shore of Coniston Water. The house is greatly extended, and Ruskin lives here until his death in 1900.

1886 W.P. Haskett-Smith is the first (known) person to climb Napes Needle, the slender rock pinnacle on Great Gable. He will repeat the climb half a century later, at the age of 74.

1895 The National Trust is formed. One of the founders is Canon Rawnsley, a parson from the Lake District.

1896 The Potter family of London, including daughter Beatrix, have a holiday in Ees Wyke, a rented house at Near Sawrey. This is Beatrix Potter's introduction to the Lake District.

1898 Henry Gaddum, an industrialist living in Manchester, has a house, named Brockhole, built on the eastern shore of Windermere. It is now a National Park Visitor Centre.

1929 Manchester Waterworks begins work on the construction of a dam in Mardale, west of Shap, which will create Haweswater Reservoir.

1937 The Forestry Commission buys the 8,000-acre/3,200-hectare Grizedale Estate near Hawkshead and begins to plant trees on a massive scale.

1941 The novelist Sir Hugh Walpole dies. For many years he owned Brackenburn, on the slopes of Catbells, near Keswick. Walpole's best-known books form a chronicle of the Herries family, in which there is much lively action in authentic Lakeland settings of past days.

1949 The Lake District is one of the 10 National Parks designated under the National Parks and Access to the Countryside Act.

1956 The National Trust opens its first Information Centre in the minuscule Bridge House at Ambleside. The house was built on a single-span bridge to serve the former Ambleside Hall as a summer house.

1967 Donald Campbell dies when his speedboat *Bluebird* breaks up after attaining an estimated 320mph (515kph) on Coniston Water. The body of Campbell was never to be recovered.

1970 The Forestry Commission uses Grizedale for a pioneering scheme to give the public unrestricted access to a state forest, and so Theatre in the Forest is established.

1974 Under local government reorganisation, the county of Cumbria incorporates Cumberland, Westmorland, Lancashire north of the Sands and a part of the old West Riding of Yorkshire.

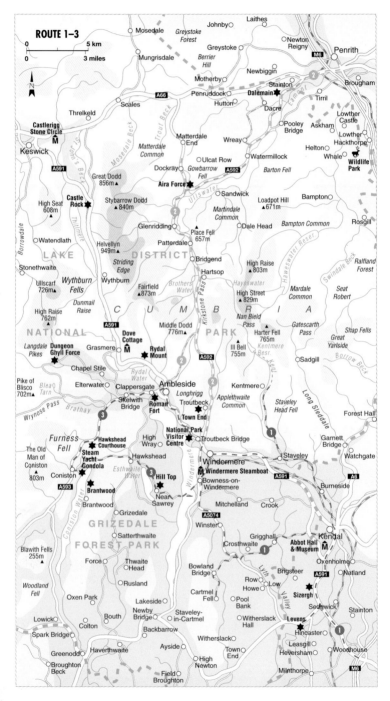

ROUTE 1–3

0   5 km
0   3 miles

N

LAKE DISTRICT
CUMBRIA
NATIONAL PARK

Laithes
Johnby
Mosedale
Greystoke Forest
Greystoke
Newton Reigny
Penrith
M6
Mungrisdale
Berrier Hill
Motherby
Newbiggin
A66
Stainton
Brougham
Penruddock
Dalemain
Tirril
Scales
Hutton
Dacre
Threlkeld
Lowther Castle
Pooley Bridge
Askham
Matterdale End
Wreay
Lowther
Hackthorpe
Castlerigg Stone Circle
Matterdale Common
Ulcat Row
Watermillock
Helton
Whale
Wildlife Park
Keswick
Dockray
Gowbarrow Fell
A592
Barton Fell
Bampton
Great Dodd 856m▲
Aira Force
Sandwick
Loadpot Hill 671m▲
High Seat 608m▲
Castle Rock
Stybarrow Dodd ▲840m
Ullswater
Martindale Common
Dale Head
Bampton Common
Rosgill
Watendlath
Glenridding
Place Fell 657m
Ralfland Forest
Helvellyn 949m▲
Patterdale
Swindale Beck
Stonethwaite
Striding Edge
Bridgend
Hartsop
High Raise ▲803m
Mardale Common
Seat Robert
Ullscarf 726m▲
Wythburn Fells
Wythburn
Brothers Water
Fairfield ▲873m
Hayeswater
High Street ▲829m
Dunmail Raise
A591
Nan Bield Pass
Gatescarth Pass
Shap Fells
High Raise 762m▲
Middle Dodd 776m▲
Harter Fell 765m
Great Yarlside
Dove Cottage
Langdale Pikes
Dungeon Ghyll Force
Grasmere
Rydal Mount
A592
Ill Bell 755m
Kentmere Resr.
Sadgill
Chapel Stile
Rydal Water
Ambleside
Kentmere
Pike of Blisco 702m▲
Blea Tarn
Elterwater
Clappersgate
Longrigg
Applethwaite Common
Staveley Head Fell
Forest Hall
Skelwith Bridge
Roman Fort
Troutbeck
Wrynose Pass
Brathay
Town End
Garnett Bridge
Watchgate
Furness Fell
Hawkshead Courthouse
High Wray
National Park Visitor Centre
Troutbeck Bridge
Staveley
A6
The Old Man of Coniston 803m▲
Steam Yacht Gondola
Hawkshead
Esthwaite Water
Windermere
Windermere Steamboat
Burneside
Coniston
Brantwood
Hill Top
Bowness-on-Windermere
Brantwood
Near Sawrey
Mitchelland
Crook
Kendal
Abbot Hall & Museum
A593
Grizedale
Winster
A5074
Coniston Water
GRIZEDALE FOREST PARK
Satterthwaite
Grigghall
Crosthwaite
Oxenholme
Blawith Fells 255m▲
Force
Thwaite Head
Bowland Bridge
Row
Low
Brigsteer
A591
Natland
Woodland Fell
Oxen Park
Rusland
Cartmel Fell
Howe
Lyth Valley
Sizergh
Sedgwick
Lakeside
Pool Bank
Stainton
Lowick
Bouth
Newby Bridge
Staveley-in-Cartmel
Witherslack Hall
Levens
Hincaster
Spark Bridge
Colton
Backbarrow
Witherslack
Town End
Leasgill
Heversham
Woodhouse
Greenodd
Haverthwaite
Ayside
High Newton
Milnthorpe
M6
Broughton Beck
Field Broughton

14

Route 1

To the shores of Windermere

Levens and Sizergh – Kendal – Kentmere – Windermere – Bowness – Lyth Valley (37 miles / 60km)

Southeast Lakeland lacks the drama of upjutting and craggy volcanic rocks, such as may be seen in Central Lakeland. But, tucked away among its quieter hills are fascinating places. In the limestone country a few miles south of Kendal are Levens and Sizergh, two contrasting stately homes. Kendal, the 'auld grey town', another reference to limestone, is now by-passed which makes the place marginally quieter than it was. Real tranquillity can be found in picturesque Kentmere. This valley is a cul de sac for motorists, but the hill-walker strides briskly on.

The destination on this route is Windermere, England's largest lake. The old steamers (now running on diesel) ply the lake and take the visitor to within sight of the rock turrets of the Langdale Pikes. Bowness Bay, a bustling place which the writer Arthur Ransome referred to as Rio, has a fascinating waterfront and the country's finest collection of steamboats. The return to Kendal is through Lyth Valley, back in limestone country. The limestone gives a special flavour to the fruit of a profusion of damson trees, which are white with blossom in May and bough-bent by fruit in September and October.

15

Having left the M6 at Junction 36 for Kendal, follow the A591 as far as the intersection with the A6 then turn left for ★ **Levens Hall** (April to September Sunday to Thursday 11am–5pm). This unusually proportioned house, home of the long-established Bagot family, proclaims its great age. A 14th-century pele tower was incorporated into an Elizabethan mansion by the Bellinghams. Then a kinsman took over Levens: Colonel Graham, whose great contribution to the house was the fine furnishings, Jacobean style, set off by panelling, plasterwork and a range of paintings. Graham also commissioned the garden, which is notable for its topiary, designed by Monsieur Beaumont, the King's gardener, in 1690. The original plans have survived, so the garden is true to the original concept. Light refreshments are served in the house. A steam collection may be viewed 1pm–5pm on open days. Just across the road from Levens Hall is parkland, adorned by venerable trees and open at all times – there are public footpaths. To be seen in the park are dark-phase fallow deer and black-and-white Bagot goats.

Head back on the A6 to a sign for ★ **Sizergh Castle** (April to October, Sunday to Thursday 1.30–5.30pm), a

Levens Hall: the topiary

Sizergh Castle

Exploring Kendal

Kendal's celebrated Mint Cake

The bristly hog in Stricklandgate

The Town Hall

Norse name meaning 'Sigrid's shieling'. Once the home of the Stricklands, it is now owned by the National Trust. As at Levens, the core of the building is a pele tower, and this was extended into a fine Elizabethan house. Of special note are Elizabethan carved overmantels. On view is English and French furniture. The garden, largely 18th-century in character, has in addition a large rockery (noted for its hardy ferns) and a small lake. The grassland is kept in a natural state, and in spring and summer it is bright with limestone-loving flowers, including orchids.

Kendal (clearly signposted from the by-pass) lies just outside the Lake District National Park. This is a town with its sleeves rolled up and its motto – *Pannus mihi pani,* 'wool is my bread' – reflects its former importance. Camden, writing in 1582, saw the 'tenter fields' where cloth was stretched out to dry after being dyed, and compared the sight with 'vine orchards in Spain'. Kendal Green was the most famous local colour, achieved by mixing woad (blue) with dyer's yellow broom. One of the customers was Robin Hood. The woollen trade transformed the town and led to the construction in the 18th century of many small yards, some good examples of which remain and are worth exploring. Notice in Stricklandgate an estate agent's shop with a protruding sign, a hog with bristles, originally made when the premises were used by a maker of brushes. The main clock is at the **Town Hall**, rebuilt on a grand scale in 1825. On market days, Wednesday and Saturday, the countryfolk would jostle with those of the town at stalls in the **Market Place**.

Today, Kendal is celebrated outside the Lake District as the home of K Shoes, Provincial Insurance and Mint Cake, a slabby, mint-flavoured confection widely used by walkers and climbers but available to all. Park the car (there is a multi-storey car park) and follow one of the Town Trails, details of which are available from the Tourist Information Centre.

A broad riverside path west of the River Kent is traffic-free and leads to ★★ **Abbot Hall** Art Gallery and Museum of Lakeland Life and Industry (March to December daily, reduced hours from October). Here is an outstanding collection of fine art, including works by portrait painter George Romney (1734–1802). There are also historical displays, with a section devoted to the life and work of Arthur Ransome (1884–1967), author of *Swallows and Amazons*. Visit also the ★ **Kendal Museum**, near the railway station. This museum has imaginative displays relating to archaeology and natural history. There is a section comprising items associated with Alfred Wainwright, the celebrated guidebook compiler.

Abbot Hall sculpture

Kendal Museum exhibit

By Abbot Hall is the ★ **Church of the Holy Trinity**, which began to take shape in the 12th century and continued until it reached a grand scale through the generosity shown by the wool merchants who endowed it. One of the aisles is named after the Flemish weavers who were brought in to help the town become prosperous. The first impression on entering the building is one of vast size – the church is 103-ft (31-m) wide. Displayed on the north wall is a helmet, said to have belonged to 'Robin the Devil', the nickname of Colonel Huddleston Philipson who rode his horse into church during divine service. He was seeking but did not find Colonel Briggs, one of his Cromwellian adversaries.

K Village Factory Shopping (weekdays 9.30am–6pm, Saturday 9am–6pm, Bank Holidays 9.30am–6pm) has a handy riverside site at the south of the town and offers for sale a wide range of footwear. Diversions include a restaurant and children's play area. The **Brewery Arts Centre**, in Highgate, is a lively multi-arts complex, incorporating theatre, cinema, music, as well as the Café Restaurant, with garden patio. **Kendal Leisure Centre** (daily 7.45am–11pm) is a large modern building, serving South Lakeland. There is no charge for the use of a large car park, and facilities within the building include swimming. Many celebrities have appeared in productions at the theatre.

On leaving Kendall, avoid using the A591 north by taking a right turn onto the B5284, just beyond the old County Hall, for **Burneside**, where the water of the Kent has been used as power for mills since corn was first ground here in 1283. The industry dominating Burneside today is the paper-making concern of James Cropper, whose enterprise grew lustily in the second half of the 19th century and, by keeping up-to-date with modern means of production,

Burneside Hall

House at Hag Foot

Dorothy Farrer's Spring

St Cuthbert's Church

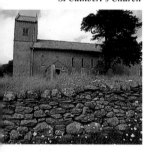

has celebrated its centenary. James himself died in 1900, but the family connection remains. One of the Croppers of national note was Margaret, a poet and hymn-writer. The most venerable building in Burneside is the Hall, now a farmhouse, where lived the 'Burnesheads'. Like many another old building in this part of Cumbria, the house was an addition to a pele tower (here somewhat ruined).

Cross a bridge over the **River Kent** and continue on a minor road by Hag Foot and Spring Foot. The woodland between the road and river is brightened in spring by clusters of small wild daffodils. **Dorothy Farrer's Spring**, a mile east of Staveley, is a nature reserve of the Cumbrian Wildlife Trust (non-members need a permit), where in more open areas the springtime flora includes bluebell, dog's mercury, lords-and-ladies and early purple orchid. Cross another bridge, about a quarter of a mile from Staveley, and turn right to follow the road into secluded ★ **Kentmere**. The road meanders amiably through a knobbly and well-wooded landscape. The glint of water indicates what remains of **Kentmere Tarn**, which shrank considerably when the valley was drained to reclaim land for agriculture. Parking in Kentmere is carefully regulated. There is usually space (for a fee) in a small field near the bridge. The road ends about a mile beyond the village, beyond which is a rough track leading to Nan Bield Pass, which connects Kentmere with the Haweswater valley.

St Cuthbert's Church sits on a ledge high above the valley and presides over a scattering of houses and farms. Amble along the little lanes and cross the tiny bridges, surrounded by an astonishing stonescape. Enormous boulders lie in fields, borne to their resting places by glacial ice. Others have been incorporated in drystone walls, demonstrating as well as anywhere the drystone waller's special skills. Keep bearing right, crossing a bridge over the River Kent and returning to the village on a lane between high walls. There are views up the valley of fells in the Borrowdale volcanic zone, including Yoke and Mardale Ill Bell, beyond which is High Street. They are part of a horseshoe of high ridges which appeal to the tougher fell-walkers. A much more gentle stroll from the Church is to Kentmere Hall, another building which developed from a simple pele tower, a sanctuary for the favoured local people. The Hall, which served as a farmhouse for a long time, can be seen from the road.

Return to Staveley and the A591, turning right for **Windermere**, which before the arrival of the railway in 1847 was the hamlet of Birthwaite, situated a mile from the lake anciently known as Vinard's Mere. A railway service still operates, though part of the station site is now occupied by a supermarket, with a café. There is also a large retail

World of Beatrix Potter

outlet of **Lakeland Plastics**, with attendant car parking and incorporating a café organised by John Tovey, the celebrated owner of Miller Howe Hotel.

Windermere is very much a Victorian town, with a variety of shops. Continue down Lake Road to Bowness and park in one of the large parking areas by Bowness Bay. **Bowness-on-Windermere** is a town around which to saunter. The promenade at **Bowness Bay** has a gala atmosphere as boats come and go at the various piers, waves lap against shingle, gulls squawk and the majority of swans seem to spend most of the day out of water, waddling about begging for food. The 'steamers' – *Swan*, *Swift*, *Teal* and *Tern* – are operated by a firm with the traditional title of Windermere Iron Steamboat Company, Ltd. Their service runs between Lakeside, Bowness and Waterhead. Windermere Lake Cruises also organises winter sailings.

The most historic building, ★ **St Martin's Church**, has an east window which consists of 15th-century glass said to have been brought from Cartmel Priory (*see page 59*). **Belsfield**, at one time the home of the Furness industrialist H.W. Schneider, is now a hotel. Schneider's iron-hulled boat, *Esperance*, can be seen, with much else, at the ★★ **Windermere Steamboat Museum** (April to October, daily 10am–5pm), which has a pleasant setting on the lakeside half a mile north of Bowness. The museum has the world's finest collection of steamboats, many afloat, some under cover. Of special interest is *Dolly* which is the world's oldest mechanically powered boat – it was launched in 1850. Weather permitting, steam-launch trips are organised on Windermere.

Occupying a central position at Bowness is **The World of Beatrix Potter** (open 10am–6.30pm in summer, 10am–4pm in winter), an exhibition which tries to create the atmosphere of walking through her books and meeting her characters. A tearoom has been added.

19

Bowness-on-Windermere

Windermere's steam heritage

Biskey Howe, which is reached by following the steep Helm Road and then going left for a few yards, provides a magnificent view of the lake and, in clear weather, many of the high fells.

From Bowness, follow the A5074 (which begins opposite the Church) into the **Lyth Valley**, *lyth* being a Norse word referring to the long slope leading up to the limestone plateau of Whitbarrow. Although it has an A classification, the road through the Lyth Valley has an easy-going manner and offers long views over Windermere.

Two miles from Bowness, in a knobbly countryside of little fields and scattered homes, lies **Winster**, with a much-photographed, white-walled post office in a house dated 1600. Its environs are a riot of flowers in summer. Just beyond Winster, the name of a roadside hotel, **Damson Dene**, draws attention to a famous product of the Lyth Valley, the damsons, which have a nutty flavour. Ripe by September, some are eaten immediately, others are preserved as jam – and yet more go to make gin. In May it's worth driving down the valley and back again to see the glory of damson blossom, which in a good year gives an impression of a light fall of snow.

20

Bowland Bridge

Near Damson Dene, an unclassified road on the right leads to Bowland Bridge. Continue up the hill beyond the bridge, where a signpost indicating ★ **Cartmel Fell Church** is seen. In summer, the church and its yard are tucked away behind a screen of leaves. The building dates back to the early 16th century, when it was a chapel-of-ease in the parish of Cartmel, a village about 7 miles (11km) away. The furnishings include a three-decker pulpit and fascinating pews, one (for Cowmire Hall) seemingly fashioned from the old chancel screen.

Pews in Cartmel Fell Church

Return to **Damson Dene** and take the road that goes as straight as an arrow to **Crosthwaite** ('clearing where a cross was raised') on the northern side of the Lyth Valley. There is no Lyth Beck, just two little rivers, one called Pool and the other Gilpin. This part of the Lake District is in delightful contrast with the austere fell country. There are relatively small fields, lots of trees and some hedges as well as walls.

Crosthwaite Village House

Follow the signs for Kendal on an unclassified but well-surfaced road. The road climbs over **Scout Scar**, the name *Scout* coming from the Norse *skuti*, meaning a steep cliff. The name is accurate: Scout Scar has a fearsome series of crags and an almost level ridge walk extending south for well over a mile. Park the car in the car park at the summit of the road, cross the road and follow a path along part of Scout Scar to a **mountain indicator** nicknamed 'The Mushroom' because of its distinctive roof.

The road leads from Scout Scar back to Kendal.

Route 2

Ullswater and the Kirkstone Pass

Penrith – Glenridding – Kirkstone – Ambleside – Kirkstone – Dacre – Penrith (52 miles / 84km) *See map on page 14*

Ullswater stretches from craggy volcanic fells to an altogether softer landscape resting on friable Skiddaw slate. The fells assembled around the upper reach appear to leap straight from the water, like mountains from a Norwegian fjord. There was once a passion, on the part of those with taste and leisure, to shatter the silence and listen to the echoes. The Duke of Portland mounted some brass guns on a boat. One who heard about it suggested that the Duke might 'let a few French-horns and clarionets be introduced.' Unlike other lakes, Ullswater has two pronounced bends, giving it a shape rather like a dog's leg. The name is Norse, meaning Ulfr's lake – although which Ulfr gave his name to the lake is hard to say, as the name was common among the Norse settlers.

Kirkstone Pass

Kirkstone Pass takes its name from a large pointed rock, said to resemble a kirk. The road, which crests at 1,489ft (454m), is the A592, which is kept open throughout the winter when some other high Lakeland passes are left to the snow-dogs. Early tourists who wrote about their experiences on Kirkstone Pass chilled their hearers. Celia Fiennes (1698) was 'walled on both sides by those inaccessible high rocky barren hills which hang over one's head in some places and appear very terrible.'

On the route described here, Kirkstone is crossed twice, the second time being from south to north, when the views are most dramatic.

Ullswater

Penrith Castle

Lying just off the M6, **Penrith** has about it a ruddy tinge from red sandstone. The town name relates to a crossing point of the Eamont, the outflow of Ullswater. The market tradition which began in the 13th century had a modern expression in the creation of a new auction mart near the big M6 roundabout. The 14th-century **Castle** is a picturesque stump, complete with grassed-over moat, in a park near the railway station. No charge is made for a visit.
★ **St Andrew's Church**, which is Georgian in style, dates from 1722. In the churchyard are the upreared stones collectively known as the **Giant's Grave**, which is associated in legend with an ancient Cumbrian king.

In the Penrith area are early earthworks. The Romans had an important fort at Brougham, a mile or so down the road towards Appleby. Just off the A6 south of Penrith is the Estate of the Lowthers, Earls of Lonsdale, whose family name was bestowed on the River Lowther.
★ **Lowther Leisure and Wildlife Park** (March to September) has various attractions spread over 150 acres (60 hectares) of deer-haunted parkland. The **Lakeland Bird of Prey Centre** (March to October) has a diverse collection of hawks, eagles, owls and falcons and offers daily falconry displays (12.30pm, 2pm and 4pm).

Lakeland Bird of Prey Centre

Leave town by the Keswick road (A66) and at a roundabout bear left (A592) for Pooley Bridge and Ullswater. The mansion seen to the right of the road, 3 miles (5km) from Penrith, is **Dalemain** (Easter to mid October Sunday to Thursday 11.15am– 5pm), home of the Hasell family since 1679. Dalemain is really three houses in one: it is Georgian in outward appearance, the facade hides an Elizabethan house, and at the core of the building is a Norman pele tower. The tearoom is in a large medieval hall. A herd of fallow deer occupies a walled park behind the house.

Letting off steam at Lowther

Where the A592 comes in sight of the lake, bear left for **Pooley Bridge**, which has a backdrop in a wooded hill called **Dunmallet** (*dun* indicating a hill fort). A fast-flowing river, the Eamont, is a tributary of the Eden (car park by the river, near the narrow road bridge).

Ullswater, not quite 8 miles (13km) long, has a sinuous appearance and a setting which gets progressively more grand with the passing miles. It was on the shore of this great lake that William and Dorothy Wordsworth saw the 'dancing' daffodils. Dorothy Wordsworth jotted in her journal her impressions of 'a few daffodils' close to the water-side. She placed the spot 'beyond Gowbarrow Park' (presumably to the south of the junction between the A592 and A5091 to Dockray). Wrote Dorothy in 1802: 'They grew among the mossy stones about and about them; some rested their heads upon these stones as on a pillow for weariness; and the rest tossed and reeled and danced, and seemed as if they verily laughed with the wind...' Between 1804 and 1807, Wordsworth adapted her prose as a poem, beginning: 'I wandered lonely as a cloud...'

Ullswater sunset

★★ **Aira Force** belongs to the National Trust, which has provided adequate car parking facilities. The falls are seen after following a good path that climbs steadily for about a quarter of a mile (0.5km). The slender waterfall tumbles a total of 60ft (18m) in a gorge flanked by trees. A small stone bridge spans the gorge. The Force has occasionally frozen, becoming an impressive icicle.

Aira Force

23

Gowbarrow Fell (a former deer park) is a place on which to wander, at relatively low elevation, with grand views of Ullswater. Walk on to Gowbarrow by going northwards from the Aira Force car park, then bearing left to the ruins of a shooting lodge. After reaching the summit, continue to the valley of Aira Beck and return via the popular footpath used by visitors to the falls.

Glenridding is said to mean 'glen overgrown with bracken'. Goldrill Beck from Brothers Water is the main feeder. Since the **Greenside Lead Mines** closed in 1962, after being worked for three centuries, the area has been landscaped. The village is almost entirely touristy, but attractive. A bridleway links up with a footpath extending to the summit of **Helvellyn** (3,118ft / 950m), a mysterious hill. The name is possibly Celtic, but no convincing derivation has been advanced. Others make a climb direct from Glenridding and (choosing dry, calm conditions) negotiate the fearsome **Striding Edge**.

★ **Ullswater Steamers** operates daily services (April to late October) in the boats *Raven* and *Lady of the Lake*. Three scheduled services from the pier at Glenridding, calling at jetties at Howtown and Pooley Bridge, and five shorter cruises (each of one hour's duration) are extremely good value. To sail on a late-morning boat to

Hartsop village

Hikers in Hartsop

Kirkstone Pass Inn

Howtown and return to Glenridding around the head of the lake on a well-defined (and very scenic) footpath is an enjoyable experience.

Patterdale, between Glenridding and Brothers Water, is named after St Patrick. A local tradition has it that the saint took refuge here after being shipwrecked on Duddon Sands in AD540. The church is dedicated to the saint, who is said to have preached in this area and baptised converts at a lakeside spring. The church features a down-to-earth request that should be noted: 'Helvellyn praises God, but please do not bring it into church on your boots.' Ann Macbeth, who lived locally from 1921 until 1948, adorned the building with splendid tapestries.

Dovedale, a tributary valley, ends on the shores of **Brothers Water**, an expanse of water under half a mile (0.8-km) long and a quarter of a mile (0.4-km) wide. The name was formerly Broad Water, but romance invests it with the sad tale of two brothers who drowned when ice broke beneath them. This area is owned by the National Trust. From a car park near the outflow of the lake there is a pleasant walk to the vicinity of ★ **Hartsop Hall**, a massive 15th-century structure. On the opposite side of the main road, the village of ★★ **Hartsop**, with 17th-century buildings, reclines in a motoring cul de sac. A track continues into the Hayeswater Valley, under the massive bulk of High Street. The place-name *Hartsop* means 'valley of the hart', which is apt, for red deer from the 'forest' at Martindale are seen in the area. Hartsop has a workaday farm and some dwellings with 'spinning galleries', where (it is said) spinsters spun wool from the fell sheep.

Kirkstone Pass is something special in a region rich in superlatives, though the crossing can be dreary in wet or misty weather. Near the summit is **Kirkstone Pass Inn**,

which has evolved from a building dating from the late 15th century. The thick-walled, heavy roofed building looks across to the face of Red Screes. There are easier ways than the Screes for anyone wishing to gain the 2,541-ft (775-m) summit of Middle Dodd. A path from the car park leads northwards for about half a mile to where 'the kirk stone', a 10-ft/3-m boulder stands on an eminence near the road.

On the way down to Windermere, make a diversion to ★★ **Troutbeck** village, with its fascinating assembly of 17th- and 18th-century buildings. The **Mortal Man** is an inn with a sign relating to an especially strong ale: *Thou mortal man, who liv'st by bread, / What is it makes thy nose so red? / Thou silly fool, that look'st so pale, / 'Tis drinking Sally Birkett's ale.*

Troutbeck and the Mortal Man

Several roadside wells in Troutbeck are dedicated to saints. At the southern end of the village, and appropriately named **Townend**, is a superb house, cared for by the National Trust (April to October, Tuesday to Friday, Sunday and Bank Holiday Monday 1–5pm or dusk if earlier). Townend was built by a yeoman in the 17th century and lived in by the Browne family, generations of whom furnished it with an array of exquisitely carved wooden furnishings. ★ **Troutbeck Church**, by the road, has an east window which was the work of a famous trio – Edward Burne-Jones, William Morris and Ford Maddox Brown. Morris was assisted by the others when they were having a Lake District holiday.

Townend

Continue on the A592 towards Windermere, but look out for a sign relating to ★★ **Holehird**. The mansion, now a Cheshire Home, is not open to the public, but the gardens are maintained by the Lakeland Horticultural Society and can be viewed. They include a wide range of rockery plants and a tree, Davidia, which produces handkerchief-like bracts in spring.

At the roundabout on the A591, go right for Ambleside and after passing through **Troutbeck Bridge** and along a stretch of road flanked by mature beeches, look out for a sign to the left for the ★★ **National Park Centre (Brockhole)** (April to early November daily 10am–5pm). The grounds, with their splendid views of Windermere and the Langdale Pikes, are open throughout the year. A large pay-and-display car park is handy for the main buildings, and access and assistance are available for disabled visitors. The formal gardens include shrub roses, herbaceous borders and a scented garden. Brockhole offers audio-visual presentations, drystone walling, exhibits and displays. There is a splendid bookshop and a café. Brockhole has a suite of offices from which the Cumbrian Wildlife Trust is administered.

Troutbeck Church window

Ambleside:
the House on the Bridge

Glass-blowing workshop

Ambleside has been described as the hub of the wheel of beauty. Roads radiate into the central valleys, and Windermere Lake Cruises operates from Lakeside, a mile away. Ambleside is a mainly Victorian town of splendid slate buildings built by craftsmen. The spired Victorian **church** contains a mural relating to a local custom, the Rushbearing, which takes place in July (*see page 64*). The diminutive **House on the Bridge**, beside Rydal Road, spans the beck and is an information centre run by the National Trust. It is said to have been built by a Scotsman to avoid paying ground rent, but in reality it was a summerhouse adorning the grounds of the old Ambleside Hall. Close by is the former **glass-blowing workshop** of Adrian Sankey, and higher up the beck is an old **corn mill** complete with waterwheel. Market day is Wednesday, when stalls are set up in King Street. They augment a wide variety of shops and innumerable eating places.

From Ambleside head back to the Kirkstone Pass, via the steep road known as **The Struggle**, which starts opposite the large car park on Rydal Road and crawls up a steep gradient to Kirkstone Pass Inn on the A592. The views northward from the pass are magnificent. Upsoaring fellsides, littered with boulders, frame a picture of Brothers Water and the high fells east of Patterdale.

Motor on through Glenridding to a point just beyond Watermillock and turn left on an unclassified road, following the signs to **Wreay** and **Dacre**. Dacre is something special, being genuine, with no tourist ploys, and having a history which boggles the mind. The church is believed to have been the site of Dacore, a monastery mentioned in Anglian times by the Venerable Bede, who relates that a young man whose eyelid was swelling at a fearful rate had it touched with a lock of the hair of St Cuthbert and within a few hours had been cured. **Dacre Castle** (not open to the public) dates from the mid-14th century. It became the property of the Hasell family in 1723 and was then restored. A further restoration took place in the 1960s, when it became the home of Bunty Kinsman. Her amusing account of life at Dacre Castle was published in 1971 under the title *Pawn Takes Castle*.

At Dacre, you can go bear-hunting. At the corners of the graveyard at ★★ **Dacre Church** are stone effigies of ★★ **bears** which may, indeed, have adorned the castle. The bear stones are much eroded, but you may pick out a bear leaning on a 'ragged staff' (northwest of the churchyard), then the bear attacked by a creature (a lynx?) on its back, and finally the bear reaching back to grab the cat. The last bear is in the course of consuming its attacker. The Norman church stands on a Anglian site.

From Dacre, head for the A66 or the A592 to Penrith.

Bear effigy at
Dacre Church

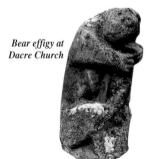

Route 3

*John Ruskin's House at
Coniston*

Tarn Hows and Beatrix Potter Country

**Ambleside – Coniston – Tarn Hows – Hawkshead –
Sawrey – Windermere Ferry – Ambleside (20 miles /
32km)** *See map on page 14*

Those who think of Lancashire as being an area of dingy
towns with forests of mill chimneys might reflect during this journey that for many centuries before local government was reorganised in 1974 most of the area being
visited belonged to the Red Rose County – yet it is a glorious area of gentle hills, lakes and tarns, woodland, white-
walled farms and cottages. During a royal visit to the Lake
District, the Queen had afternoon tea at one of the little
whitewashed farms in Yewdale. Beatrix Potter met Peter Rabbit at Near Sawrey. The Victorian steam-yacht *Gondola* still cruises on Coniston Water to a regular timetable
and with a full head of steam. It calls at a pier at Brantwood, home to John Ruskin, the great Victorian thinker,
writer, artist and social reformer. Brantwood overlooks
Coniston Water and the Coniston Fells, one of the finest
views in England. Tarn Hows, which is frequently portrayed in books and on picture postcards as an example
of scenic Lakeland, has a haunting beauty despite being
in a sense man-made. The water is retained by a dam to
regulate its flow to the Monk Coniston estate. The trees,
upstart conifers, impart a resinous smell.

Loughrigg seen from the water

The A593 from **Ambleside** runs to the south of the sprawling, multi-turreted **Loughrigg Fell**, which is deserving of
a visit by itself. Obtain a leaflet at the Bridge House, Ambleside, relating to a 2½-mile (4-km) nature saunter on the
Fell, from which there are stunning views of Ambleside

and Rydal Water). The A593, in its meanderings, offers glimpses of the **River Brathay** (a Norse name for a broad river), which gathers up near the Three Shires Stone on Wrynose Pass and has transfusions of cold beck water from Little Langdale before offering a white-water spectacle near **Skelwith Bridge**. Parking is available to those patronising a gift shop and café. It is but a short walk to ★ **Skelwith Force** ('the noisy fall').

Yewdale

The road to Coniston now climbs between tracts of indigenous woodland at the verge of the crags of the Borrowdale volcanics. A roadside tarn on the right, backed up by conifers, gives the journey a backwoods flavour. The road dips into **Yewdale** (valley of the yew trees) which is owned by the National Trust. Wordsworth described the valley as 'An area level as a Lake and spread / Under a rock too steep for man to tread. The 17th-century farms are architecturally outstanding…' This is part of Arthur Ransome Country. The author belonged to a Leeds family, and the holidays of his boyhood were spent at Nibthwaite, near the outflow of Coniston Water. He was in the Yewdale area on a protracted holiday in 1908 when he came up with the story of *Swallows and Amazons*. One of the Yewdale farms is described in his novel *Winter Holiday*. The great hill **Wetherlam**, which dominates the valley, appears in *Swallowdale* and *Pigeon Post*.

Coniston Water

At **Coniston**, the presiding mountain is **The Old Man of Coniston** (2,635ft / 803m), which can be climbed on a well-marked route from the village by good walkers who, in chancy weather, have waterproof clothing. On the way up are many traces of mining and quarries for slate.

The presiding spirit at Coniston is John Ruskin, whose grave at ★ **St Andrew's Church** has a Celtic-style cross of Tilberthwaite stone, with a design (reflecting his many interests) devised by his secretary and good friend, W.G. Collingwood, another notable writer. Collingwood shares the glory with Ruskin in the ★★ **Ruskin Museum**, founded in 1900 and recently renovated (Easter to October daily except Saturday 11am–1pm and 2pm–5pm). The Museum is a few minutes walk from the church. Ruskin lived at Brantwood, east of Coniston Water, from 1819 until his death in 1900.

Ruskin's Grave

★★ **Brantwood** (mid-March to mid-November daily 11am–5.30pm, winter Wednesday to Sunday 11am–4pm) may be reached by road from Coniston (B5285) or, as indicated, by the steam yacht ★★ *Gondola*, which sails from Coniston Pier (signposted from the village) daily from 30 March until 3 November, weather permitting. The first sailing is at 11am (12.05pm on Saturday). If the weather is chilly, visitors can find shelter in the upholstered saloon.

Gondola glides through the water

This 1859 steam launch, the design for which was approved by that great arbiter of good taste, John Ruskin, was well-known to Arthur Ransome. His *Swallows and Amazons* was inspired by memories of boating on Windermere and Coniston Water. In two of his books, the *Gondola* became a houseboat. In real life it lay wrecked in Nibthwaite Bay for many years but was rescued by the National Trust and given an extensive restoration. Notice how the steam engine is responsive and quiet as the craft glides through the water.

A view of ★★★ **Tarn Hows**, north-east of Coniston, appears on virtually every calendar with a Lake District content. It is, in effect, man-made, and almost as familiar to a Lakeland enthusiast as the back of the hand. Even so, like the *Mona Lisa*, it might be visited time and again without mental weariness. Tarn Hows is reached by turning left from the Coniston–Hawkshead road (B5285) down a signposted byroad. A one-way system is in operation. There is adequate car parking provided by the National Trust, including a car park for disabled people that is much closer to the lake. A good footpath leads around the tarn, which was created about a century ago by building a dam and merging three tarns. The views of the Lakeland fells from the southern side of the lake, where the path takes to higher ground, are quite magnificent.

Tarn Hows

29

The exit road links with the Coniston-Hawkshead road. Turn left for Hawkshead. Near the junction with the Ambleside road is the ★ **Courthouse** (April to October daily 10am–5pm, key from the National Trust Shop, The Square, Hawkshead). This distinguished building is all that remains of a range of 15th-century manorial buildings associated with Furness Abbey. The Courthouse holds a standing exhibition relating to local life.

The Courthouse

Traffic has virtually been eliminated from the narrow streets and squares of **Hawkshead**. A reflection of the popularity of this wonderful little town, with its white-painted buildings, its narrow streets, yards and alleys, is the difficulty in finding space in the large car park. Hawkshead folk are keen on their heritage, and one shop specialises in a sort of pastry called a wigg.

The Grammar School

The ★★ **Grammar School** (founded 1585 by Archbishop Sandys but no longer used as such) is open to the public (April to October weekdays 10am–12.30pm and 1.30pm–5pm, Sunday 1–5pm). William Wordsworth received part of his education (1779–87) here, and he carved his initials on his desk. He lodged with Mistress Tyson either at Hawkshead or nearby Colthouse (there were Tysons in both places). He enjoyed walking and also raven-watching, recalling: *Oh! when I have hung / Above the raven's nest, by knots of grass / And half-inch fissures in the slippery rock...*

The poet Wordsworth now takes second place at Hawkshead to Beatrix Potter, whose spirit broods over several shops specialising in her books and related souvenirs and at the National Trust's ★ **Beatrix Potter Gallery** (April to October Sunday to Thursday 10.30am–4.30pm, admission by timed ticket). The Gallery occupies offices used by William Heelis, the solicitor husband of Beatrix. There is a display of books, papers, furnishings and a selection of original water-colours that were painted by the multi-talented Beatrix.

St Michael's mural and view from the church

The most prominent building in Hawkshead is ★ **St Michael's Church**, a large and handsome structure indicative of 15th-century prosperity, the inner walls adorned with murals and painted texts dating from the 17th century. The Church is the venue for musical occasions on certain summer Sundays. When viewed from the knoll,

the white-washed houses of the old town appear to huddle. Each building seems to have its unique style, which is why a person is inclined to return again and again to Hawkshead. One never tires of the place.

A short distance along the lakeside road is a right turn for Grizedale and the Theatre in the Forest (*see page 59*). **Esthwaite Water** (which means 'lake by the eastern clearing') has a length of 1½ miles (2km). The Young Wordsworth frequently began a new day by walking round the lake, being back in time for school; he also skated on Esthwaite Water. The lake has a pastoral setting and now sustains a trout fishery.

Esthwaite Water

Follow the B5285 from Hawkshead to **Near Sawrey**, so called because it is closer to Hawkshead than Far Sawrey. Beatrix Potter's first Lake District holiday with her family was at Wray Castle, a Victorian spoof edifice near the northwestern shore of Windermere. On the next visit, in 1896, the Potter family stayed at Ees Wyke, a large and pleasant house at Near Sawrey. She was so fond of this quiet part of what was then North Lancashire that she used the royalties from her first book, *The Tale of Peter Rabbit,* published in 1900, to purchase ★★ **Hill Top** (National Trust, April to November Saturday to Wednesday and Good Friday 11am–5pm). Being one of the major attractions of the Lake District, and relatively small, a limited number of visitors will be admitted at any one time. The approach to Hill Top, a former farmhouse, is through a National Trust shop, then along a garden path (a way often taken by Beatrix). The house, which was not her home after her marriage, contains furniture and china. Visitors may recognise the kitchen range and the main staircase, both of which are illustrated in *The Tale of Samuel Whiskers*. When she married William Heelis, a rather solemn Lakeland solicitor, Beatrix was 47 years of age. They resided in **Castle Cottage** in Near Sawrey (not open to the public).

31

Beatrix Potter's Hill Top

Follow the road to **Far Sawrey**. The Claife Crier Bar at a local inn relates to a ghost who, in monastic times (when the Windermere ferry was a rowing boat) terrified both ferrymen and potential passengers by hailing the ferry. On its arrival, no one was to be found. The ghostly crier was laid to rest by monks from Furness Abbey. The large car-carrying **Windermere Ferry** that now plies the lake is held on course by metal cables stretched from shore to shore. The journey takes only a few minutes, but years ago, a London lady who intended to visit the Lake District for the first time wrote asking to book a berth for the crossing. The ferry does not operate in winter.

Return to **Ambleside** by the A592 and the A591.

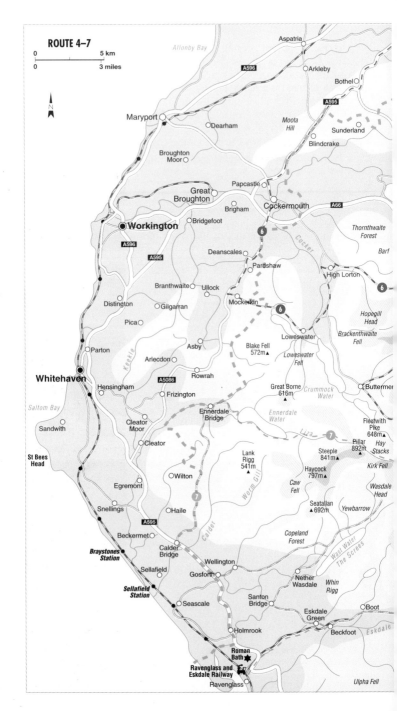

ROUTE 4–7

0 ———— 5 km
0 ———— 3 miles

N

32

Allonby Bay

Aspatria
Arkleby
Bothel
A596
A595
Maryport
Dearham
Moota Hill
Sunderland
Blindcrake
Broughton Moor
Papcastle
Great Broughton
Brigham
Cockermouth
A66
Workington
Bridgefoot
6
Cocker
Thornthwaite Forest
Barf
A596
A595
Deanscales
Pardshaw
High Lorton
6
Branthwaite
Ullock
Mockerkin
6
Hopegill Head
Distington
Gilgarran
Loweswater
Brackenthwaite Fell
Pica
Blake Fell 572m▲
Loweswater Fell
Asby
Arlecdon
Great Borne 616m
Crummock Water
Parton
Rowrah
A5086
Buttermere
Whitehaven
Hensingham
Frizington
Ennerdale Bridge
Ennerdale Water
Liza
7
Fleetwith Pike 648m▲
Saltom Bay
Sandwith
Cleator Moor
Cleator
Lank Rigg 541m▲
Steeple 841m▲
Pillar 892m▲
Hay Stacks
Kirk Fell
St Bees Head
Wilton
Worm Gill
Haycock 797m▲
Caw Fell
Wasdale Head
Egremont
Snellings
Haile
Seatallan ▲692m
Yewbarrow
A595
Beckermet
Calder Bridge
Wellington
Copeland Forest
Wast Water
The Screes
Braystones Station
Sellafield
Gosforth
Nether Wasdale
Whin Rigg
Calder
Sellafield Station
Seascale
Santon Bridge
Eskdale Green
Boot
Holmrook
Roman Bath ★
Beckfoot
Eskdale
Ravenglass and Eskdale Railway
Ravenglass
Ulpha Fell
Keekle
Carder

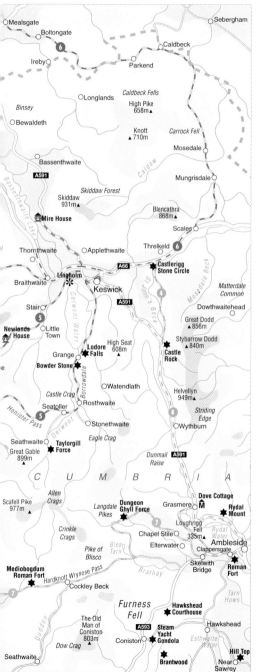

Keswick Pencil Museum

Encounter near Caldbeck

Ravenglass and Eskdale Railway

Grazing at Castlerigg

Route 4

Keswick, Grasmere and the Vale of St John

Thirlmere – Dunmail Raise – Grasmere – Rydal Water – Ambleside – Vale of St John – Keswick (31 miles / 50km) *See map on pages 32–33*

Keswick, northern capital of the Lakes, presides over Derwent Water and Bassenthwaite Lake, with Skiddaw (locally pronounced *Skidder*) clearing the 3,000-ft / 900-m contour. Climbing the fell is not difficult, just protracted, and people usually start from Millbeck, near Applethwaite, or from Latrigg. Charles Lamb enthused after climbing it in 1802: 'O its fine black head & the bleak air a top of it, with the prospect of mountains all about & about, making you giddy…' Blencathra, its neighbour, provides a backdrop for the sprawling village of Threlkeld.

Keswick Market Place and the Moot Hall

Keswick retains a strong Victorian appearance which belies its age. The name is Old English for 'cheese farm', the K being a dash of Old Norse. View Derwent Water in its setting of fells and woodland and then try to imagine the conditions over 1,300 years ago, when Hubert, a Christian saint, became a hermit on one of the islands. About AD550, Kentigern, hearing that 'many among the mountains were given to idolatry', erected a cross as a sign of faith' at Crosfeld (Crosthwaite). Leland (1540) arrived to find 'a lytle poore market town cawled Keswike'. Soon afterwards, the place was industrialised with the arrival of German miners. They were employed to seek gold, but in the end they mined copper. Graphite, discovered in the 16th century and mined in the Seathwaite valley at the head of Borrowdale, has always been useful, but with the arrival of the pencil, Keswick assumed world eminence as a centre of pencil production. As the Romantic Age developed towards the end of the 18th century, Keswick became allied with tourism. Coleridge noted in 1800 that 'for two thirds of the year we are in complete retirement – the other third is alive & swarms with Tourists of all shapes & sizes & characters.'

Keswick has a **Moot Hall** (market hall) which has the grand lines and spired tower of a church (with a one-handed clock) and rises from a traffic island in an area almost entirely devoted to tourism. The Moot Hall itself holds a tourist information centre. Keswick's ★★ **Museum and Art Gallery** (Good Friday to the end of October, daily except Monday 10am–noon and 1pm–4pm) has a handy situation in Fitz Park and is a good starting point for anyone with an interest in local traditions. The museum has a delightful Victorian flavour, and among the exhibits are a scale model of the Lake District (1834) and a 'Bell, Rock and Steel Band'. Literary connections are stressed through letters and manuscripts. On display are letters by Wordsworth and Southey. The manuscript of some of Hugh Walpole's novels interest an increasing number of admirers of his work called *The Herries Chronicle*.

Museum and Art Gallery

Greta Hall, the home of Samuel Taylor Coleridge in 1800–03 and of Robert Southey in 1803–43, is part of Keswick School and not normally open to the public.

Of wide interest is the ★★ **Cumberland Pencil Museum** (daily 9.30am–4pm). Displays relate to the mining of graphite and the making of pencils.

35

Pencil Museum drawing

Leave Keswick on the A591 and call at ★★★ **Castlerigg**, which is well signposted. Here, set on a hill with a wondrous panorama of greater hills all around, 48 grey stones form an oval (not a true circle) about a hundred feet across. Other stones form a rectangle to the east of the main group. Was Castlerigg the centre of a tribal territory? No one knows. To the Victorian tourists, this was a haunt of Druids, but Castlerigg probably dates back to the much earlier Bronze Age. Wordsworth wrote in 1818 of *a dismal cirque / Of Druid stones upon a forlorn moor.*

Castlerigg stone circle

The A591 unfolds under the gaze of high fells. **Castle Rock** *(see page 39)* guards the entrance to the Vale of St John on the left. The Dodds, crowning the skyline, are to the north of mighty **Helvellyn** (3,116ft / 950m; *see page 23*). Steepness does not deter modern walkers, and **Thirlspot Inn** on the left is one of several starting points from which an ascent of Helvellyn might begin.

Nature trails are to be found in the woodland on either side of **Thirlmere**. A car park that is also a good observation point is situated on the right hand side of the A591.

Thirlmere, 4 miles (6km) long, may be circumnavigated by the motorist. A plaque on the dam commemorates the beginning of work on the reservoir (22 August 1890) which grew from two small lakes, Leathe's Water and Wythburn Water. The dam holds the water to a depth of 50ft (16m) – more than the level of the natural lakes. Thirlmere feeds the water-taps of Manchester, some 90 miles (56km) away. At times of low water, the bare shore-line may look unsightly, but the plantations that once stood like battalions of soldiers at attention are more varied now. Red deer inhabit the woodlands west of the water, and they summer on the open fells beyond.

★★ **Wythburn Church** (pronounced *Wyburn*, meaning a valley where willow trees grow) is visible on the eastern side of the A591. The building, long, low and predominantly 17th-century, has retained the old Lake District flavour. Near the church, visitors making the steep ascent of Helvellyn park their cars.

Wild poppies by the roadside

Rejoin the A591 for a crossing of the watershed at **Dunmail Raise**. This ancient pass between Thirlmere and Grasmere has been improved for motorists by a stretch of dual-carriageway. A cairn at the top, between the carriageways, explains the name of the pass. It marks where Dunmail, the last king of Cumberland, was defeated in AD945 by Edmund, King of Northumbria.

Dunmail Raise was, until 1974, on the border of Cumberland and Westmorland. There is a good view of the rugged 'mane' of **Helm Crag** (right) from the lay-by on Dunmail Raise. Reaching the summit demands rock-climbing skill and nerve. Wainwright, in his pictorial guide to the area, left a space on which he might write the date of his ascent, but he never managed that last awkward bit. Coachmen driving four-in-hands from Windermere to Keswick entertained tourists by giving names to unusual rocks, the most notable being the **Lion and the Lamb**, at the southern end of the ridge.

The Raise allows people to hear as well as see further. In the early 19th century, during the Peninsular War, Thomas De Quincey (one of the Wordsworth coterie) and William Wordsworth walked up the Raise from Grasmere, at about midnight, to meet the Keswick carrier and the London papers. They had advance notice of his approach when Wordsworth lay on the ground and listened. De Quincey said this was so he might 'catch any sound of wheels that might be groaning along at a distance'.

Grasmere village

Grasmere, the heart of Wordsworthshire, has several large car parks, one of which is adjacent to Stock Lane and quite close to the field in which the **Grasmere Sports** have been held in August for over 130 years. There were traffic problems when Beatrix Potter visited the Sports in

1895, for she was a late arrival 'and had difficulty in finding friends among the crowd of carriages'. Lord Lonsdale, arriving via Kirkstone Pass in a yellow-painted coach, took special interest in the Cumberland and Westmorland style of wrestling, on which he was an authority. Wordsworth effusively wrote that Grasmere was 'the loveliest spot that man hath ever found'. Grasmere (the lake, that is, complete with island and rowing boats) lies in what he called 'a mountain urn'. The Vale of Grasmere is virtually ringed by shapely fells, of which the most prominent is Helm Crag. The novelist E.M. Forster, who stayed in the village in the summer of 1907, liked the place though he said 'it rains all night and every day, but not always all day.'

Grasmere Lake

There is plenty for non-literary day trippers to do, for Grasmere is half full of little shops. The more studious visitors make for ★★ **St Oswald's Church**, which still is (as it was in Wordsworth's time, 1799–1813) a structure *of rude and antique majesty [with] pillars crowded and the roof upheld / By naked rafters intricately crossed / like leafless underboughs in some thick wood*. The annual Rushbearing on the Saturday nearest 5 August (*see page 64*), was a feature of the Poet's day, for he saw children, each with a garland, walking through the still churchyard, noting that the garland was carried 'like a sceptre and o'er-tops the head of the proud bearer.' Pilgrims form respectful knots before the Wordsworthian graves.

37

★★★ **Dove Cottage** (daily 9.30am–5.30pm, closed 24–26 December and from 8 January to 4 February), the Wordsworth home during the early, highly creative years, stands just to the east of the A591, in an area known as Town End. The white-washed cottage is now hemmed in by much later buildings. The Wordsworths had a view directly over Grasmere and on to the fells, as Dorothy noted in December, 1801: 'We played at cards – sat up late.

Dove Cottage and garden

The moon shone upon the water below Silver-How… Wm lay with his curtains open that he might see it.'

Dove Cottage has its own little car park, but as the space is always in keen demand it is recommended that the large car park in Stock Lane (B5287) is used, from where it is but a few minutes walk to the cottage. The cottage was Wordsworth's home (and that of his sister Dorothy) from 1799–1808. It was a time dedicated to plain living and high thinking. Dove Cottage is particularly appealing in cold weather, when a bright fire burns in the grate. In the adjacent ★★ **Wordsworth Museum**, a barn conversion, a permanent exhibition recounting the Wordsworth story is backed up by special exhibitions. Dove Cottage has a reciprocal discount scheme operated with Rydal Mount and Wordsworth House at Cockermouth.

Grasmere and Rydal Water are connected by a footpath along **Loughrigg Terrace**. The path can be reached directly from Dove Cottage along a causeway by the road that offers unhindered views of the lake and Helm Crag or via a wood called Bainbriggs, a favourite pre-tea walk of the Wordsworths. Alternatively, use the large car park near the church, and walk around the other side of the lake. After a little road work, a well-used footpath is found which leads to the south of the two lakes.

Rydal Water

Rydal Water, which is smaller than Grasmere, is a reedy lake, with several islands and a population of waterfowl. Red squirrels might be seen in the larches. The view for much of the year is given a ginger hue by the dead bracken fronds. Across the lake, once secluded but now in its own little lay-by of the A591, is **Nab Cottage**, a blob of white against the lower slopes of Nab Scar. Thomas De Quincey lodged here and then married Peggy Simpson, daughter of his landlord. Wordsworth thought that Thomas could have done better, but the happy couple remained happy. The De Quinceys moved to Wordsworth's old cottage at Grasmere, and into Nab Cottage came Hartley Coleridge, the son of Samuel Taylor Coleridge. The literary connection thus continued.

Wordsworth's study, part of his house at Rydal Mount

★★ **Rydal Mount** (daily in summer 9.30am–5pm, in winter 10am–4pm) is at the head of the village, near the start of a footpath leading back to Grasmere. William Wordsworth lived here from 1813 until his death in 1850. A descendant now owns the house. After a brief introductory talk, visitors may wander around house and a 4½-acre (2-hectare) garden, which was landscaped by Wordsworth. ★ **Rydal Church**, a 19th-century structure with a memorial to Dr Thomas Arnold, his wife and son Matthew, is adjacent to ★ **Dora's Field**, which Wordsworth bought and gave to his daughter, Dora. Unhappily, she died and the field reverted to Wordsworth. Pilgrims

in April walk between expanses of daffodils and narcissi – if the sheep haven't got to them first. **Rydal Hall**, home of the le Flemings in Wordsworth's day, is now a conference and study centre for Carlisle Diocese. The gardens are open to the public, and a footpath to Ambleside passes through the park.

Motor into **Ambleside** (*see page 26*), follow the town's one-way system and take the A593 through Clappersgate. Turn right just before Skelwith Bridge and the junction with the B5343, up a signposted road that crosses **Red Bank** (which has a splendid view of Grasmere lake) and back to Grasmere town. Take the A591 back over Dunmail Raise to Thirlmere.

Ambleside pier

The B5322 leaves the A591 for the **Vale of St John**. The crag on the right is known as **Castle Rock**, and it greatly impressed early tourists. William Hutchinson (1774) compared it with 'an ancient ruined castle' which, as they drew near, 'changed its figure, and proved no other than a shaken massive pile of rocks.' Walter Scott, shown the rock and having read Hutchinson's account, wrote *The Bridal of Triermaine*, a poem in which King Arthur finds the castle deserted, rouses it with a bugle blast and brings it back to life, complete with 'a band of damsels fair'.

John Ruskin

39

To motor down this vale when the high fells are powdered with snow is to enjoy an alpine spectacle, for the eye goes directly to **Blencathra** (2,847ft / 868m), which appears to block out half the sky. John Ruskin, who climbed Blencathra in 1867, thought of it as 'the finest thing I've yet seen, there being several bits of real crag-work and a fine view at the top over the great plain of Penrith on one side, and the Cumberland hills, as a chain, on the other. Fine fresh wind blowing, and plenty of crows.'

Woolly jumpers

Two miles down this pastoral valley, look for a roadside sign, ★★ **St John's Church**. A narrow road leads to the church, which sits snugly behind yew trees in the shadow of a steep hill. A church on the site was mentioned in a document dated 1554, but the present structure dates only from 1845. One of the finely-lettered tombstones in the yew-adorned churchyard relates to John Richardson (1817–86), whose poems in the Lakeland dialect are still much enjoyed.

At **Threlkeld**, go left to Keswick, where (if time allows) there is a change of mood at **Beatrix Potter's Lake District** (April to June, September and October daily 10am–5pm; July and August daily 10am–5.30pm; November to March weekends only noon–4pm) in Packhorse Court. This multi-media show relates to her 'saving' 6,000 acres (2,400 hectares) of the Lake District and her contribution towards conservation.

Route 5

The Borrowdale Round

Keswick – Grange – Seathwaite – Honister Pass – Buttermere – Newlands – Lingholm (20 miles / 32km)
See map on pages 32–33

Canon Rawnsley, a Victorian parson of Keswick, considered there was 'no better five shillings worth of carriage driving at the Lakes than can be enjoyed by all who gather in the Keswick Market Place on a fine morning at ten o'clock and take their seats on any of the char-a-bancs waiting to convey them up Borrowdale, thence home by the Newlands Vale.' Able-bodied passengers were asked to walk up steep hills. On descents, a squeal emanated from a 'slipper' or wedge of wood on which a wheel rode. It was a primitive but effective braking device. Coach-drivers gave a commentary on what was to be seen and related stories of local daftness. The Borrovians (if such is the term) were said to have constructed a wall across the bottom of the valley to restrain the cuckoo and ensure everlasting summer.

Borrowdale, to many the most scenic of the Lakeland valleys, offers some demanding crags for rock-climbing and walkers move jauntily along its airy ridges.

Angling at Derwent Water

Outward bound on the lake

The B5289 is the name given to the romantic road that runs through Borrowdale to Buttermere. The road leaves Keswick to skirt **Derwent Water**, the 'queen' of English lakes, which has a maximum depth of 72ft (22m), but looks shallow. Derwent Water mirrors a range of handsome fells and also the Jaws of Borrowdale, best seen from ★★ **Friars Crag** (on the right as you leave Keswick, it is an easy walk

from the car park). As well as pleasure craft, there is a regular boat service to various jetties, and lakeside walks are well laid out. Of the islands, St Herbert's had the hermitage of a Celtic saint. Derwent Island became the home of German immigrants of the 16th century, whose skills as miners were needed to recover local copper.

Near the head of Derwent Water, behind the Stakis Lodore Swiss Hotel and accessible on payment of a small charge, are the ★★ **Lodore Falls**, about which Robert Southey wrote *The Cataract of Lodore* (1820), first asking how they did it then answering in a style which is now familiar to all Lakeland visitors, including: *Collecting, projecting, / Receding and speeding, / And shocking and rocking, / And darting and parting...* A visit to the falls is exciting in wet spells. It is said that an American, after looking for them for several hours, sat down and asked a passer-by, 'Say, where are the Lodore Falls?' They informed him that he was sitting on them!

Lodore Falls

Grange-in-Borrowdale (*grange* because of the granary of Furness Abbey) is reached over a narrow, double bridge. The ★ **church** is picturesque both inside and out. About a mile from Grange on the road running west of Derwent Water stands **Brackenburn**, a private house that was owned by Hugh Walpole, author of *The Herries Chronicle* and many other novels. Though private, its main features can be seen from the road, and above the garage, where he had a study decked by 30,000 books, is a blue plaque commemorating Walpole's association. To him, this was a 'little paradise on Cat Bells', the hill looming beyond. Water drawn from deep in the fell has the tingle effect of good wine.

Church cross at Grange

41

Grange is a good point from which to walk, just for a mile or two, beside the river and through the famous Borrowdale oak woodland. The species of oak is the north-country 'sessile', a reference to the stalkless acorns. The **River Derwent** has a green appearance – the water is pure and the bed of the river is composed largely of pieces of greenish slate.

River Derwent

Continue on the B5289 to where there is parking near a sign heralding the ★★ **Bowder Stone**, an enormous boulder with a length of 62ft (19m) and a height of 36ft (11m). A wooden ladder with rails, fixed against the side of the Stone, gives access to its summit.

The road continues, pent-in between **King's How** (named after Edward VII) and ★ **Castle Crag**, which looms above the oakwoods on the west bank and is best approached from Grange. Climbing its steep scree slope is not to be undertaken lightly, but with care visitors can reach a supreme vantage point looking over the oak-wooded valley, Derwent Water and Skiddaw.

Rosthwaite, a village with a car park and toilets, has a Post Office with shop that is popular with visitors. The village is at the start of a footpath leading over the fell to the remote hamlet of **Watendlath**. From Rosthwaite there is ready access to the riverside, with a walk up the dale to **Seatoller**. Of special interest, west of the river and between Rosthwaite and Seatoller, is **Johnny Wood**, in which there is a nature trail. **Stonethwaite** to the left is a hamlet worth exploring, and walking up the dale for a short distance brings **Eagle Crag** into view. Rosthwaite and Stonethwaite were named by Norse settlers for the amount of stone lying about, all of which had to be cleared before cultivation.

The road to Seatoller

The eagles of Eagle Crag were persecuted, as were ravens. Churchwardens' accounts reveal that a bounty was paid on dead birds. The traveller Gray, visiting Grange-in-Borrowdale in 1769, heard from a farmer how the previous year he plundered the eyrie of the golden eagles: 'He was let down in ropes to the shelf of the rock on which the nest was built, the people above shouting and holloaing to fright the old birds, which flew screaming round, but did not dare to attack him'.

Seatoller is a cluster of attractive buildings, some erected for quarrymen when the Honister mines were first opened. The National Park authority converted a barn into a base with displays and study facilities, and craft workers visit the base to give demonstrations.

A reminder of local mining

THE BUTTERMERE
AND WESTMORLAND
GREEN SLATE CO. LTD.

HONISTER MINES AND QUARRIES
BORROWDALE   BORROWDALE
Nr KESWICK CUMBRIA

The dale peters out at **Seathwaite Farm**, a mile south of Seatoller, left down a side road. The wettest inhabited farm in England (125 inches / 3,175mm a year), four generations of Edmondsons have farmed Seathwaite. There is roadside parking, a sheep farm, trout farm and a small café. A short walk from Seathwaite Farm is **Stockley Bridge**, a packhorse-type bridge on the route from Borrowdale to Wasdale. There is also a track from Seathwaite barn across the valley to a river bridge, from which an approach may be made to waterfalls in **Sour Milk Ghyll**. On the hillside are remains of the old graphite mines (which must not be explored because of potential danger). When a pure form of graphite was discovered here in the 16th century, it had various uses. Being rare and of practical value, including making metal castings and cannon balls, it was treated like gold. In the early 19th century, guards were posted at the mines and workmen were searched before they left. Graphite was eventually to be used extensively in Keswick's pencil industry.

The Honister Pass

Able-bodied men taking the Borrowdale Coach Round in the 19th century had to walk up **Honister Pass** (1,190ft/362m) from Seatoller. Canon Rawnsley, arriving at the head of the pass, saw **Honister Crag**, which 'gleams

at us as if some great earth painter had been grinding up grey slate and mixed it with emerald and begun to wash in his colour from skyline to the valley bottom'. The slate quarried up here was composed of the compacted dust and ash from volcanic activity. A rough track now runs up the side of Honister Crag, and there is little to indicate that the whole fell is honeycombed by shafts and galleries. For a time, it was customary to pack slate on long sledges and run with the sledges down the screes to the roadside below. The sledgeman then had to climb back with his sledge for another load.

Looking back from the pass into Borrowdale

Rugged country

Fell walkers park their cars beside Honister Pass when following a comparatively easy route to the summit of **Great Gable** (2,949ft / 899m). On Remembrance Sunday, many gather on Great Gable to remember those who fell in two world wars. They stand beside a memorial to those members of the Fell and Rock Climbing Club who were victims in the conflicts.

The road descends from the heights of Honister to **Buttermere** lake, which is reached at Gatesgarth Farm at the foot of shapely **Fleetwith Pike** (2,126ft / 648m). A car park just across the road from the farm is handy for those who wish to explore the dalehead. Others go on to the **Fish Inn** at Buttermere village, where (wrote Joseph Budworth in 1792): 'If you are fond of strong ale, I must tell, Buttermere is reckoned famous for it.' The tale is told of Mary, the 'Buttermere Beauty'; she was the daughter of a landlord of the Fish Hotel in the early 19th century and was noted for her looks. Budworth saw her: 'She brought in part of our dinner, and seemed to be about fifteen. Her hair was thick and long, of a dark brown, and, though unadorned with ringlets, did not seem to want them; her face was a fine oval, with full eyes and lips as red as vermillion; her cheeks had more of the lily than of the rose.' Mary attracted the attention of a 'gentleman' who announced

Buttermere blooms

Buttermere Church

Wainwright Memorial

PAUSE AND REMEMBER
ALFRED WAINWRIGHT
FELLWALKER, GUIDE BOOK AUTHOR
AND ILLUSTRATOR
WHO LOVED THIS VALLEY.

LIFT YOUR EYES TO HAYSTACKS
HIS FAVOURITE PLACE.

1907 - 1991

himself as the Hon. Alexander Hope MP, brother of the Earl of Hopetoun. They were married in 1802. Unfortunately, he turned out to be John Hatfield, an imposter, bigamist, forger and bankrupt. His iniquities led to him being hanged at Carlisle. The Buttermere Beauty later married a local farmer, and they had a large family.

It is possible to walk around Buttermere lake, though one of its features, a tunnel cut in living rock, has been closed for safety reasons. When Rawnsley did the 'Buttermere Round', a break was arranged for lunch at Buttermere village. There was time to visit 'the tiny church, with its twelve steps in memory of the Apostles'. On a window ledge in **Buttermere Church** is a plaque in memory of Alfred Wainwright, the most famous of fellwalkers and author of the *Pictorial Guides* to the Lake District fells. Look through the window on a clear day and the fell named **Haystacks** is in view. Wainwright's ashes were scattered on Haystacks at his special request.

Follow the road up past the church for the third leg of the journey. **Newlands Hause** used to warm up the coach horses, and the most athletic passengers would be asked to walk to lighten the load. **Newlands** is a secluded valley, almost a basin among fells, with lots of farms and two diminutive hamlets, Stair and Littletown, the last-named being well-known to Beatrix Potter, who included drawings of it in *The Tale of Mrs Tiggy Winkle*. The mine levels driven into the flanks of **Cat Bells** and **Maiden Moor** were worked in the days of Queen Elizabeth I. They yielded copper, lead and even a little gold.

The road to Portinscale and back to Keswick passes ★ **Lingholm Gardens** (April to October, daily), where 40 acres (16 hectares) of rhododendrons and azaleas have a woodland setting. This superb garden is also noted for its magnolias and maples. Refreshments are available.

Route 6

Back o' Skiddaw and on to Cockermouth

Keswick – Mungrisdale – Caldbeck – Cockermouth – Crummock Water – Whinlatter (60 miles / 97km) *See map on pages 32–33*

Old Skiddaw tops the 3,000-ft (900-m) contour and sprawls over an area of 14 sq miles (36sq km). Walkers who cross the fell or follow a good path from near the old Sanatorium at Threlkeld to Skiddaw House sample an austere landscape 'Back o' Skidder'. Almost every creature that breathes is a sheep. Astonishingly, Skiddaw House, built for the use of shepherds, is now a youth hostel in season, with an outroom available to anyone in need of shelter, a can of soup and a bivvy-bag.

Skiddaw slate gives this northern fell country some grand sweeping lines, as anyone can see who follows a cul de sac from Mosedale beside the River Caldew to what remains of mining days at the highly-mineralised hill called Carrock Fell. Those who walk the hills can look far south into the valley containing Thirlmere. In the churchyard of Caldbeck lie the mortal remains of huntsman John Peel, who inspired a world-famous song. (Incidentally, he had a coat so *gray* – the undyed wool of the Herdwick sheep). Westwards lies the market town of Cockermouth and classic Lake District terrain, with soaring fells admiring their reflections in Loweswater and Crummock Water.

The A66 east of Keswick is dominated by **Blencathra** (2,847ft / 868m, *see page 39*), a fell empurpled by flowering heather in late summer. Walkers who use the Threlkeld car park and start with a walk through the fields at the foot of the great hill usually pick the path on the arête that leads directly to the summit. In a strong wind, avoid this route. Coleridge, one of the Lakeland Poets, appreciated the power of moving air: *On stern Blencathra's perilous height / The winds are tyrannous and strong; / And flashing forth unsteady light / From stern Blencathra's skiey height, / As loud the torrents throng!*

Leave the A66 for **Mungrisdale**, where the ★ **church**, dedicated to St Kentigern, is an architectural treasure dating from the 18th century, long, low, whitewashed and containing a three-decker pulpit dated 1679. The clerk sat on the lower deck while the parson took the service from the second deck and preached from the top deck. Drive on through Mosedale into an area which gives the 'feel' of the big country Back o' Skiddaw. The valley itself is scenic, with the atmosphere of a Scottish glen – boulders, heather and a brawling beck, crossed at one point

Mosedale farmhouse

45

Mungrisdale Church

by a private bridge that gives access to a walk to **Bows-cale Tarn**, in a grand setting of fells. Where the road peters out, there is the remains of a mine at **Carrock Fell** (2,174ft / 662m). In 1857, Carrock was visited by Charles Dickens and Wilkie Collins, though local people had told them no visitors ever went up that hill. The two men had arrived on a wet day, and at the top, in mist and rain, they had a magnificent view of nothing.

Caldbeck

On to **Caldbeck** (meaning cold stream). This area is a vast sheep range also frequented by some of the stocky, dark fell-type ponies once ridden by the shepherds and used for light farm work. Caldbeck, built largely of limestone, is on the northern boundary of the Lake District National Park. Ask locally for directions to the ★ **Howk**, a limestone gorge popularly thought of as a place for fairy revels, hence the alternative name Fairykirk. Caldbeck drew much of its former prosperity from industries powered by the fast-flowing River Caldew. Local people used to brag about their wealth: *Caldbeck and Caldbeck Fells / Are worth all England else.*

Gravestone of John Peel

John Peel – the huntsman, d'ye ken – was born at Park End in 1776 and interred in the Caldbeck churchyard in 1854. Hunting symbols are found on his gravestone, which is big, of a light tone and not far from the Church door. The words which have gone round the world in the song *D'ye Ken John Peel* were composed by John Woodcock Graves, a great friend of Peel who emigrated to Tasmania. Peel's portrait is kept in the **Oddfellows' Arms**. *John Peel* was first sung 'in the snug parlour' of Graves's house in the year 1824, to the tune of a Border rant called *Bonnie Annie*. An improved version of the music was devised in 1869 by William Metcalfe, the choirmaster of Carlisle Cathedral. Metcalfe's tune survived.

Wordsworth House

Take the B5299 over the back of the fell country to the A595 and turn left for **Cockermouth**, a market town that stands back from Lakeland proper, its red sandstone buildings emphasising its peripheral status. The town sits at the confluence of the Rivers Cocker and Derwent and was given a market charter in 1221. The broad, tree-lined main street is relatively quiet,having been by-passed by the A66. At the western end is ★★ **Wordsworth House**, where the poet was born in 1770 (25 years after the house was built). Wordsworth's father was steward to the Lonsdales. Now a National Trust property, the house is open to the public (April to October weekdays 11am–5pm and some Saturdays, closed Sundays). Seven rooms are furnished in the original style, and some of the poet's personal effects are displayed. The garden is extensive, and a terraced walk leads down to the Derwent.

Cockermouth Castle was built in the 12th century to repulse Scottish raiders. During the Civil War, it held out for Parliament in 1648. The castle has suffered more from decay than from warlike forces. One of the wings, re-built in the 19th century, is still occupied. A memorial win-dow to Wordsworth is to be found in **All Saints Church**, a Victorian structure with a 180-ft (55-m) spire and eight bells in the belfry.

★ **The Lakeland Sheep and Wool Centre**, in Egre-mont Road, is open all year round (sheep are on show from mid-February to Easter daily at 10.30am, noon, 2pm and 3.30pm; otherwise Wednesday to Sunday). The centre is a hands-on opportunity for visitors to meet some of Cumbria's most famous residents. Nineteen dif-ferent breeds of sheep are on view during the indoor pre-sentations, and sheepdogs are put through their paces in a 300-seat arena. The centre has a café restaurant.

Lakeland Sheep and Wool Centre

The **Cumberland Toy and Model Museum**, in Banks Court, Market Place, exhibits mainly British-made toys from around 1900 to the present day (February to No-vember daily 10am–5pm).

Another Cockermouth attraction

47

Several villages in the Cockermouth area have produced famous men. Fletcher Christian, who mutinied on the *Bounty*, was born at Moorland Close in 1764. John Dal-ton of atomic theory fame was born in Eaglesfield in 1766. On the coast, **Maryport** harbour has been restored and has an attendant museum. **Whitehaven** is a stimulating town, handy to St Bees Head, a redstone promontory with seabirds. At the **Helena Thompson Museum** in Work-ington are displays of silver, glass, furniture, dresses and the social history of the town (April to October, Monday to Saturday 10.30am–4pm; otherwise Monday to Satur-day 11am–3 pm). **Workington Hall** – a refuge for Mary Queen of Scots during her last night of freedom in May, l568 – is a ruin, but plaques give visitors a flavour of this impressive hall's long history, dating from the 14th cen-tury, when it was simply a pele tower.

Maryport Harbour

Leave Cockermouth on the A5086 and take a left turn for **Loweswater** ('leafy lake'). The road follows the shore of the mile-long lake and then on another half mile to the village of Loweswater, which is almost shadowed by **Mell-break** (1,676ft / 511m). **St Kentigern's Church** is not as old as the name suggests, having been rebuilt in Vic-torian times. Take the B5289 through Lorton Vale and drive to Buttermere village and back to enjoy fine views of **Crummock Water**.

Continue along the B5289 to High Lorton, and turn right at the B5292 for **Whinlatter Pass**, passing through Thorn-thwaite Forest with its ★★ **Visitor Centre**. A vantage point by the road offers a good-weather view of **Bassenthwaite Lake** and Skiddaw. The lake is 4 miles (2.5km) long, a half a mile (0.8km) wide and 51ft (16m) deep. There is a noisy side (the west) and a relatively quiet side. The noise is from traffic speeding on the A66 to and from the industrialised towns of the West Cumbrian Coast.

Just before the A66, take the old road through Braithwaite and Thornthwaite to where the **Swan Hotel** stands in a wooded area. Looming above the hotel is the hill known as **Barf** (the pronunciation of Barugh, a north-country surname). The hotel rewards with a pint of ale a volunteer who regularly whitewashes the Bishop of Barf, a large stone marking the place where a man who fancied himself as a skilled horseman came to grief when attempting to ride up that side of the mountain. The area below the Bishop is mainly scree and unsound. A path approaches the summit from the side and back.

Mirehouse

Drive around the top of Bassenthwaite Lake via the B5291 and head back to Keswick on the A591. About 3½ miles (5km) before Keswick is the ★★ **Mirehouse** (30 March to 2 November; grounds 10am–5.30pm daily; house 2pm–4.30pm Sunday and Wednesday; house also Friday in August). This large family home, built in 1666, was last up for sale in 1688. It was extended in 1790, the additions including a stylish porch of red sandstone. Mirehouse has many connections with celebrities in the world of literature and art. John Spedding lived here; he was a school friend of Wordsworth at Hawkshead. Tennyson stayed at Mirehouse in 1835 and was reported to 'admire the country near the lakes very much, but could dispense with the deluges of sapping rains.'

On open afternoons at Mirehouse, piano-playing can be heard. Some visitors stroll to the edge of Bassenthwaite Lake and look around **St Bega's**, an ancient lakeside church that was restored in Victorian times.

Before driving into Keswick, visit ★ **Crosthwaite Church**, on the northern edge of the town, where the gateway is adorned by Celtic motifs designed by Canon Rawnsley (1851–1920), vicar of Crosthwaite for many years. Crosthwaite took its name from the cross erected in a clearing by St Kentigern (*see page 34*). The first church would have been of wood and thatch, but traces of the Norman building that succeeded it are to be found in the north-aisle wall of the present church. The 16th century was a good time for Keswick, judging by the extensions made at the church. In 1844 the place was completely restored under the direction of Sir George Gilbert Scott. Look for the marble figure of Robert Southey (1774–1843), poet laureate at the time of Wordsworth who, incidentally, wrote an epitaph – and succeeded his friend as poet laureate. Southey's grave is on the north side of the church.

Route 7

The Western Lakes

Ambleside – Great Langdale – The High Passes – Wasdale Head – Ennerdale (60 miles / 97km) *See map on pages 32–33*

Ambleside Glass House Restaurant

Great Langdale doesn't have a lake, but it has all the other attributes of a picturesque Lakeland valley – a beck, green fields hatched by dry-stone walls, and mountains blocking out more than half the sky. The passes of Wrynose and Hardknott are not for the timid, but they allow a motorist to go mountaineering without special effort.

The western Lake District is out of the way but worth the effort. One of the truly great sights is the Screes beyond Wastwater, preferably lit by a setting sun, draped like giant fans from a 1,700-ft (520-m) long cliff – the southeastern buttress of sprawling Scafell. Elsewhere, the prominent features are sternness and sterility. As Thomas Wilkinson, a visitor in 1824, wrote: 'The mountains of Wast Water are naked to their base – their sides and their summits are uniform; their summits shoot up into lofty points and end in the form of pyramids.'

The Langdales

Wasdale, its Screes and the dalehead with the pyramid of Great Gable all lie at the centre of a trinity of shapely fells. They make most sensitive people babble – but not Wordsworth, who described Wastwater matter-of-factly as 'long, narrow, stern and desolate'. Coleridge, in 1802, infused plenty of life and colour into his description of the Screes as 'consisting of fine red Streaks running in broad Stripes thro' a stone colour – slanting off from the Perpendicular, as steep as the meal newly ground from the Miller's Spout… like a pointed Decanter in shape, or an outspread fan.'

Kirkstone Galleries

Start from **Ambleside** (*see page 26*). At Borrans, near the head of Windermere, stood a Roman fort named **Galava** (National Trust). It was commented on by Camden, who bravely entered these parts in 1586. He saw 'the carcase as it were of an ancient city with great ruins of walls, and of buildings without the walls still remaining scattered about.' Now there is just an expanse of grass. To visit the area is an appropriate prelude to the first part of this route, which takes in the high passes of Wrynose and Hardknott, where a Roman road connected them with Ravenglass, a natural harbour on the Cumbrian coast.

Follow the A593 from Ambleside to **Skelwith Bridge**, calling at the **Kirkstone Galleries**, on a site near the bridge and beside the river. The Galleries (April to October 10am–6pm, November to March 10am–5pm) feature crafts associated with Lakeland stone, offering a variety of products. The workshops, with craftsmen at work, are adjacent to the Gallery.

At Skelwith Bridge (*see page 28*), leave the A592 for the B5343 and Great Langdale, which bursts into view near **Elterwater**. Across the common and beyond the woodland rise the **Langdale Pikes**, one of the most distinctive landforms in the district. Elterwater has a large car park near the river bridge and a smaller car park (property of the National Trust) on the west side of the common, which is a grazing area for Herdwick sheep. The evidence of slate-quarrying is everywhere, and a terrace of slate dwellings overlooking the common is unusual and attractive. There are few visible remains of the old gunpowder factory that supplied the quarries. In its place is a large and attractive timeshare complex.

Great Langdale proper is entered at **Chapel Stile**, in which the most prominent building is **Holy Trinity Church**. The church stands up a hill as though on a ledge,

Elterwater

Elterwater's village shop

which means that church-going requires physical as well as spiritual stamina. In the churchyard is the grave of G.M. Trevelyan, author of *English Social History*, a classic book published in 1944.

Beyond the village, Thrang Crag and the residues of slate quarrying are prominent. So is a terrace of houses and holiday flats. A road to the quarry begins near a craft shop, but it is unwise to explore redundant quarries without taking local advice and wearing a stout helmet.

The Langdale Pikes dominate the dale with the impact of a Sphinx. Three fells are seen, these being **Harrison Stickle** (the highest, at 2,414ft / 736m), **Pike o' Stickle** and **Pavey Ark**, and there are five summits in the group. The Pikes can be ascended, with some effort, from the New Dungeon Gill Hotel. Car parking seems ample, but in summer it is in the keenest demand. Near the foot of Pavey Ark's 600-ft (200-m) cliff is Stickle Tarn which, dammed in 1824, provided a constant head of water, via the river, for the gunpowder works at Elterwater.

The road leaves the valley near **Wall End Farm**. Notice how large are some of the boulders in and beside the beck. The road climbs to **Blea Tarn**, in a secluded little valley, where an attractive farmhouse was the home of Solitary, a character in one of Wordsworth's poems. A car park to the left of the road is useful for anyone who wishes to use the footpath across the little valley. The car park is handy, too, for Blea Tarn, where there are trees and (a surprise) a grove of rhododendrons.

51

On reaching **Little Langdale**, turn right for the **Wrynose Pass**, sometimes referred to as 'pass of the stallion', the implication being that a strong horse was needed to negotiate it. Wrynose has a steep gradient, taking little time to attain 1,289ft (393m), and a reasonably good surface (because of work done after World War II, when it was used for military training). At the summit is a stone pillar marked 'Lancashire' but known as **Three Shires Stone**. Here, before local government reorganisation in 1974, the counties of Cumberland, Westmorland and Lancashire were on nodding terms.

Wrynose Pass

The road descends to the head of the **Duddon Valley**, where **Hardknott Pass** (more fearsome than Wrynose) begins its course to Eskdale with a steep gradient and a quick succession of hairpin bends, delivering the motorist to an elevation of 1,291ft (394m). Care is needed during the descent. Beside the road, on a plateau looking into Eskdale, are the considerable remains of ★★ **Mediobogdum**, a Roman fort. There is space beside the road on which to park the car. Wordsworth, in one of his sonnets about the River Duddon, pictured an eagle flying over the ruins of a fort 'whose guardians bent the knee to Jove

Duddon Valley

'Ratty'

Muncaster Water Mill

and Mars'. **Eskdale**, though lakeless, extends with a quiet charm down to **Boot**, where the holiday spirits of many are buoyed up by the the **Ravenglass & Eskdale Railway** (affectionately known as Ratty).

At **Eskdale Green**, a narrow, unclassified road leads to **Santon Bridge** and on to **Nether Wasdale**, where the grandeur of **Wasdale** is unfolded. Alternatively, travel down to **Ravenglass**, where the Romans took advantage of a fine natural harbour. Here, England's oldest narrow-gauge steam railway offers the chance to visit, in novel fashion, **Muncaster Water Mill**. The railway operates daily until early November, with special days around Christmas and winter weekends, tel: (01229) 717171.

On the journey through Wasdale, firstly there is a view of **Wastwater**, which has a cold, blue appearance. It is almost sterile and the least changed of the great lakes since they were formed by the scouring of glacial ice. Wastwater is very deep and in places extends below sea level. The famous **Screes**, to which reference has been made, are part of a 3-mile (5-km) cliff on a fell known as Illgill Head (1,998ft / 608m). The road, in places unfenced, stays close to the northern shore of the lake and is fringed by sheep-cropped herbage and gorse, the yellow blossoms of which enliven the district in spring. Where visitors stop, there are usually black-headed gulls, their raucous cries instilling a little life into the rockscape.

The glorious scenery unfolds slowly as the journey proceeds. On the left is **Yewbarrow**, which is not much higher than 2,000ft (600m) but has a 'mountain' appearance. It is a long drag over grassy terrain to get to the summit, which is a vantage point for the really big fells of the dale-head. However, they can also be seen and admired from a car. At centre stage is **Great Gable** (2,949ft / 899m),

Wastwater

in the form of a rugged pyramid, which confirms everyone's impression of what a mountain should be. Gable's companions are **Kirk Fell** (2,360ft / 802m) to the left and **Scafell Pike** (3,206ft / 978m). At least, that's how it seems from the floor of Wasdale Head, though Scafell Pike is the highest peak in England.

Wasdale Head is a surprise to those who expect a dale to get narrower and rockier as it comes to its head. For here is a great tract of alluvial soil, thatched in lush green, overlaid by an intricate (and altogether fascinating) pattern of drystone walls. So much stone was cleared from the land that a lot was simply heaped up and walled around. The tiny ★★ **church**, one of the smallest in England, has timbers said to have come from a shipwrecked vessel. The outline of Nape's Needle, Gable's celebrated rock pinnacle has been scratched on one of the windows. A conquest of the Needle is obligatory in the career of a Lake District climber. To this end Wasdale attracted a host of Victorian climbers, some of whom exercised on the gable end of a local barn. The **Wastwater Hotel** has rooms decked with photographs of early climbers. There is also a Ritson Bar, named after Will Ritson, an archetypal dalesman who told 'tall' stories and was fond of saying that Wasdale had the biggest mountain, the deepest lake and the biggest liar – himself (*see pages 64 and 65*).

Wasdale Church

53

On the way from Wasdale, stop in **Gosforth** to see the 14½-ft (4.5-m) carved ★★ **Viking Cross** in the churchyard at St Mary's. Made of red sandstone and somewhat worn after nine centuries of wind and rain, the cross was raised when paganism was giving way to Christianity. Images from Norse mythology and Christian symbolism are portrayed. At **Calder Bridge**, leave the A595 for a hill road to **Ennerdale Bridge**. A stone circle to the right on the moor towards the end of this section is, indeed, a Victorian spoof. A road, ending in a car park, connects the village of Ennerdale Bridge with the end of the public road by **Ennerdale Water**.

Viking Cross detail

Ennerdale Water

Walkers on the **Coast to Coast** route (St Bees to Robin Hoods Bay) and day-trippers with plenty of time and energy walk to the head of Ennerdale. The lower reaches were desecrated by water authority and forestry interests, the period of the massed trees dating from 1927 before the Forestry Commission became 'environmentally friendly'. More recently, the effect has been softened by maturing timber, sensible management and some amenity planting. As the Backwoods are left behind the towering peaks of Great Gable, Kirk Fell, Pillar and Steeple come into view with Hay Stacks rising behind a solitary building, ★ **Black Sail** youth hostel.

The A5086, then A66, ensure a quick return to Keswick.

Route 8

The Southwest

Grange-over-Sands – Ulverston – Duddon Valley – Wrynose – Grizedale – Cartmel (66 miles / 106km)

Morecambe Bay

The tide sweeps across Morecambe Bay with the speed of a good horse. It performs pincer movements round the sandbars and spreads itself languidly over the mudflats. In a short time, what had been a damp desert is an arm of the sea, choppy and chilling. Then, with another turn of the tide, the Bay is once again what someone called a 'wet Sahara', though this is no desert. On the mudbanks thrive small creatures that sustain dense flocks of wintering birds. Years ago, the bay at low tide would be alive with fisherfolk from the villages who, with horses and carts and tackle, sought cockles, mussels, dabs, flukes and, of course, the famous Morecambe Bay shrimps.

North of the Bay are limestone hills and beyond them the high fells. A journey in this area is ever-varied. Grange-over-Sands is a good starting point because it grew with tourism and is served by rail and bus. After breakfast, a stimulating experience is to walk along the promenade, hearing the cries of gulls and seabirds, or beside the duck-thronged pond in the parkland on land reclaimed when the Furness Railway stabilised the coast with its tracks. This route runs through Furness, up the glorious Duddon Valley, over the pass into Little Langdale and back via Grizedale Forest and Cartmel Priory.

Grange-over-Sands: station and shops

Grange-over-Sands is on the B5277 – which loops off the A590 halfway between Levens and Newby Bridge. It began as a monastic 'grange' or granary, but a stimulus to the development of Grange took place when it was connected to the rail network in 1857. The Victorian and Edwardian holidaymakers it attracted, and that muddy beach, ensured it would not grow into a major holiday resort. It would remain a place for discerning folk, on whom it thrives today. The architecture of the station, the formal park with its bird-busy lake, and the elegant shops, with their cast-iron canopy, appeal to those who remember a more gracious age. A clock tower makes a brave attempt to give the town a focal point.

Those of an athletic inclination find pleasure in heading upbank from the clock tower, following the signs for ★ **Hampsfell**, with its restored shelter-cum-observation point that offers a fine-weather view of distinction, taking in Ingleborough and other Yorkshire peaks as well as those of the Lake District. A footpath, with striking views of the Bay, leads from Grange to neighbouring **Kents Bank**.

Drive to Allithwaite, and from there follow the B5277 westward to Flookburgh. It is also possible to drive to the start of a nature reserve, the narrow, hedge-bordered road from Allithwaite negotiating a level crossing on the railway. The promontory to the left is ★ **Humphrey Head**, the highest point on the west coast between Wales and St Bees Head. **Flookburgh**, a mile or so inland from the bay, was a village of horse-and-cart fisherfolk, who operated on the bay at low tide. Shrimps were caught by a trawl net with a beam. As the beam approached a shrimp in one of the channels, the shrimp jumped – straight into the net. Cockles by the ton were once transported in sacks from the railway station at Cark. Notice, as you drive towards **Cark**, the next village, that the weather-vane on the church is a gilded fish, not a cockerel.

Fish weather-vane at Cark

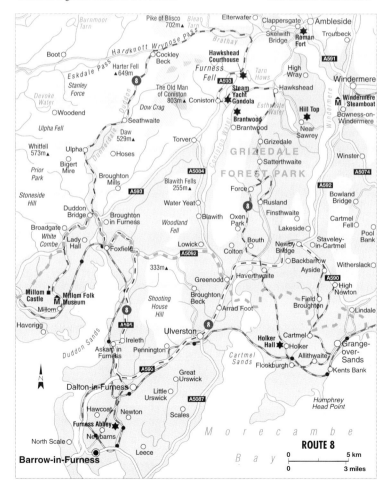

ROUTE 8

| 0 | | 5 km |

| 0 | | 3 miles |

Holker Hall gardens

★★ Holker Hall (April to October, daily except Saturday 10am–6pm) lies just beyond Cark. The splendid home of the Cavendish family dates from 1871, replacing a previous building that was gutted by fire. Red sandstone was used to create a building which has a markedly Elizabethan style. Part of the old 17th-century house remains. It was the home of the Preston family, benefactors of Cartmel Priory. Holker is set in an award-winning garden which, in turn, lies within a deer-haunted park. Joseph Paxton, designer of the Crystal Palace, was invited to plant the 'monkey puzzle tree' (Chilean pine). It has reached an enormous size and is pinned down for stability, having once been blown down in a gale.

Lakeland Motor Museum

Outbuildings at Holker hold the **★ Lakeland Motor Museum** (April to October, daily except Saturday 10.30am–5pm). More than 150 classic cars are on view, together with an exhibition on the Campbell water-speed legend and *Bluebird*, a boat with a revolutionary design.

The road from Holker unfolds in long straight stretches in an almost flat landscape that consists of sappy grass or indigenous woodland, beloved of naturalists. The road joins the A590, and a turn left leads beside the **Leven Estuary**, where the overflow from Windermere mixes with the salty tide. Continue through Greenodd and on to **Ulverston**, which has a distinctly nautical flavour. The ship canal from the bay was built by John Rennie in 1796, but is now in effect a static water tank for Glaxo-Wellcome. The 'lighthouse' on Hoad Hill is actually a scaled-down model of the Eddystone lighthouse, built in 1850 in memory of the naval administrator and traveller Sir John Barrow (1764–1848), a native of the town and founder of the Royal Geographical Society. Hoad Hill may be climbed from Ulverston in under half an hour. **Cumbria Crystal** in Lightburn Road (normal working hours year round except Bank Holidays, the last week in July and the first week in August) is a major tourist attraction. Ulverston has become widely known for its **Laurel and Hardy Museum** (Easter to October, daily except Wednesday and Sunday, 10am–5pm). Stan Laurel, the English half of the famous movie duo, was a native of the town.

Laurel and Hardy Museum

Continue on the A590 to **★ Swarthmoor** (mid-March to mid-October, Monday to Wednesday and Saturday 10am–noon and 2pm–5pm), an Elizabethan hall of major interest to Quakers. George Fox, founder of the Society of Friends, was a frequent visitor from 1652 when the hall was owned by Judge Thomas Fell and his wife, Margaret. When the Judge died in 1658, the immunity he had secured for Quakers lapsed and they were persecuted. Margaret later married George Fox, and both suffered hardship and imprisonment for their beliefs.

At **Dalton-in-Furness**, the so-called Castle is a 14th-century tower with monastic links standing in the main street. It was built by the Abbot of Furness when Scottish raiders were troublesome. On the dissolution of Furness Abbey (*see below*), some of its attractive red sandstone was transported to Dalton to repair the tower, which became a prison and courthouse. Dalton had its economic heyday in the 19th century with the growth of ironstone mining and the lifting of 7 million tons of ore from local mines. Today, the town is more widely known for the **South Lakes Wild Animal Park** (April to September 10am–6pm, otherwise 10am–dusk). This is described as Lakeland's only zoological park, and the approach to it is indicated by tourist signs showing an elephant. Species on show range from free-flying parrots to Sumatran tigers.

An invitation to the zoo

Not far from Dalton, to the left of the A590 and on the edge of mighty Barrow, a short, constricted road leads under a monastic arch to the outstanding remains of rose-red ★★★ **Furness Abbey** (daily, except Sunday morning). Originally founded in 1127 by monks of the Order of Savigny, Furness later joined the Cistercians and became one of the richest abbeys in the land. The area became known as the Vale of Deadly Nightshade because of the profusion of those plants. The Abbey's extensive remains, on a 73-acre (30-hectare) site, are breathtaking. Red sandstone stands out against the green of well-manicured lawns. The nave and transepts date from the 12th century, the massive west tower from the 15th century. Everything at this affluent establishment was on a big scale. The east window was huge, and the dormitory, over 200ft (60m) long, was said to be the largest of any English abbey.

57

The A595 turns northwards, with a gleam from the Duddon estuary to the west. Drive around the estuary to **Broughton in Furness** just off the A595. The name Broughton is Old English and means a farmstead or village by a stream. Now there is a settlement with a stylish market square, overlooked by fine buildings, shadowed by trees and with a set of stocks as a reminder of an old-time punishment.

Broughton in Furness

Carry on around the side of the estuary and the goose-haunted marshes, beneath the brooding giant of **Black Combe**, to the quaint little Victorian town of ★ **Millom**, a child of the Furness ironstone boom and the home of Norman Nicholson (1914–87), a poet in the Wordsworthian tradition. His bust bedecks the library, and he is deemed important enough to warrant a section to himself in the adjacent folk museum. Less than a mile from the town of Millom, beside the A5093, are **Millom Castle** (a pele tower) and a restored 13th-century **church** that hint at the pre-industrialised feel of the area.

A poet remembered

Duddon Valley cottage

The River Duddon

Bactrack along the A595, but turn left just before the narrow bridge spanning the **River Duddon**, and enter the **Duddon Valley**. The road runs high, offering views across wooded hills, which in the days of Furness Abbey provided timber for the making of charcoal and in the 18th century supplied fuel for an early **forge**, the substantial remains of which, not far from Duddon Bridge, are preserved. The iron ore was brought up the Duddon, and the forge operated using charcoal made from local woodland, which was clear-felled and burnt slowly in 'pits'. Wordsworth wrote a sequence of 35 sonnets about the River Duddon, describing it as 'majestic' and, at Duddon Bridge, making 'radiant progress towards the deep'.

The Duddon frolics between jumbled boulders and the dried fronds of bracken, providing perfect picnic areas, though being secluded the valley does not attract a great many visitors. Man has lived in these parts for several thousand years, judging by sepulchral mounds on the flanking hills from which have been taken calcified bones. Ulpha, who gave his name to a main settlement, ★ **Ulpha**, is said to have been the son of Evard. He received the manor when the land was re-apportioned following the Norman Conquest. Ulpha has a little gem of a church – Wordsworth's 'Kirk of Ulpha' – perched on a knoll beside the road and dedicated to St John the Baptist. The font is ancient, and the altar is fashioned from the wood of a fruit tree.

The hamlet of **Seathwaite** (a Norse name derived from 'clearing of the shieling', a summer pasture) has an inn. Robert Walker (1709–1802), who was curate at Seathwaite for well over 60 years, became known as Wonderful Walker because of his thrift and industry. Although on a stipend of only a few pounds a year, he had managed to accrue £2,000 by the time he died at the age of 92. His wife, who was equally thrifty, died in the same year. The curate is commemorated by a plaque in the church.

The most attractive part of Duddon Valley is where ★★ **Birks Bridge**, a single span across a gorge, enables people to pass dryshod over the swirling river. The pools have a dark green hue. Rowans (mountain ash) have rooted among the rocks. The big conifer forest to the west of the river dates back 60 years to when the Forestry Commission planted dense ranks of alien spruce. The passing years have brought some welcome changes. There are now picnic areas and other facilities for the public use.

At **Cockley Beck**, those wishing to test their motoring skill on **Hardknott Pass** (*see page 51*) cross the bridge over the Duddon. Otherwise keep straight ahead along Wrynose Bottom, source of the Duddon. Three Shires Stone offers a chance to park and stretch the legs before the steep descent into Little Langdale, having exchanged the Duddon for the Brathay (*see pages 28 and 51*).

The Duddon idyll

Join the A593 and go south to **Coniston**, following the B5285 to **Hawkshead** (*see page 30*). Just south of the village is a turning on the right to ★★ **Grizedale Forest**, developed on an 8,000-acre (3,200-hectare) estate purchased by the Forestry Commission in 1937. During World War II, Grizedale Hall was used to house prisoners, one of whom escaped and returned home, via Canada, being the only German prisoner in that conflict to make a successful escape. In the post-war period, the Commission pioneered the concept of a commercial forest to which the public is granted access to learn about the countryside and walk along waymarked paths, adorned by fascinating sculptures, the work of young artists. One of the sculptures is a representation in wood of a wild boar. From the deer museum opened in 1956 has developed a visitor centre, and the **Theatre in the Forest**, which has an international reputation, was established in 1970. Artistes of renown enjoy performing here.

Grizedale Forest: sculpture and Theatre sign

Continue to **Satterthwaite**, **Rusland**, **Booth** and the A590, where you turn left through Backbarrow and Newby Bridge to a right-hand turning for **Cartmel**. You'll notice, as the village comes into view, the upstanding and lovingly preserved ★★ **Priory**, with the curious diagonal extension to its central tower. The main fabric is original, created in 1188. Some of the gravestones on the floor relate to people who were drowned while crossing Morecambe Bay by the old low-tide route from Hest Bank. Elsewhere in the village is the well-preserved monastic gateway, which was in use from 1624 until 1790 as a grammar school. It now belongs to the National Trust and is an **art gallery and folk museum** (April to October Tuesday to Sunday 11am–5pm). **Cartmel Races** take place in an attractive parkland area.

Grange-over-Sands lies just over the hill.

59

Cartmel Priory

Cartmel Village Square

The Historic Landscape

Opposite: Sizergh Castle

Archaeology

Our knowledge of early life in the Lake District was transformed in 1947 by the discovery of pieces of chipped volcanic rock on the 2,000-ft (600-m) scree slope of Pike o' Stickle at the head of Great Langdale (*see page 51*). This proved to be the site of a **prehistoric axe-factory**, the first major Lake District industry, operating in Neolithic times, some 4,000 years ago.

Until this find, it had been thought that penetration of Central Lakeland had occurred much later. At Pike o'Stickle, and various other places in the high fell country, pieces of 'tuff', a particularly hard rock, were 'roughed out' with hammers made of granite. Then (it is theorised) they were taken to the coastal strip for final shaping. Langdale rock was traded throughout the country. The Great Cumbrian Axe was set to work to thin out the old forest, which extended far up the hillsides.

The Mesolithic folk had been hunters, their dreams haunted by such images as the red deer. In Neolithic times, people were clothing themselves with wool from the cragsheep, and burial urns were being used. In the late Neolithic and the early Bronze Age, spectacular **stone circles** were raised, the most notable being at Castlerigg, near Keswick (*see page 35*). Much smaller, but impressive in its broad moorland setting, is the Cockpit on Askham Moor. It's an easy walk from the village, near Penrith, to the moor, where the visual remains of ancient peoples are to be seen everywhere.

When the Romans swept north in the first century AD, the Lake District (like most of the North Country) was tenanted by a tribe known as the Brigantes. The most memorable of the ancient sites of the Lake District is that of a **Roman fort** beside Hardknott Pass (*see page 51*). It stood beside a road connecting Ambleside with the natural harbour at Ravenglass. The appreciable remains of the fort are on a spur of land at an elevation of 800ft (244m). Archaeologists affirm that the builders of this fort came from the area that was to become Yugoslavia.

Architecture

Pele towers, three storeys high and considered impregnable, are distinctive early stone structures, now (in most cases) forming the core of much larger buildings, as at Levens Hall, Sizergh Castle and Kentmere Hall (*see page 18*). At Burneside (*see page 18*) the pele tower, adjacent to a farmhouse, is partly ruined and we have an insight into fine details of its construction. Pele towers date from the 14th century, when local people sought protection from repetitive Scottish raids.

61

Stone circle at Castlerigg

Field studies in progress

Large houses of early date include Coniston Hall, with its cluster of circular chimneys above open hearths (to be seen after a short walk from the *Gondola*'s pier at Coniston Water, *see page 27*). The circular chimneys so highly praised by Wordsworth were not so much for show as the best way of using irregular stones.

In the 17th century, with the Border troubles over and Lakeland families having security of tenure, there was a widespread reconstruction of farmhouses. A typical 17th-century Lakeland farm was built of stone and slate wrenched from quarries near at hand, with small windows and a stout porch to protect the front door from the searching wind. There is a roughness about many farmhouses that reflects the unsuitability of local stone, but the builders did their best. Every dale has fine examples of this vernacular architecture. Some, as at Hartsop (*see page 24*) and Yew Tree Farm near Coniston have 'spinning galleries'. Most of the dalehead farms are now owned by the National Trust. An outstanding example of a Lakeland yeoman's home is Townend at Troutbeck (*see page 25*).

Apart from the typical Lakeland farms and cottages constructed, sometimes with difficulty, from the native stone and slate, the Lake District was the setting for some distinctive architectural forms imposed on it by outsiders and usually criticised by the neighbours for doubtful if not bad taste. One such structure is the Round House on Belle Island, Windermere, built on a whim by Mr English in 1774, badly damaged by fire in recent times and now in the course of reconstruction. The most famous 'odd' building in the Lake District must be the Bridge House, sitting over a stream in Ambleside, which many people falsely claim was built by a Scotsman who wanted to avoid paying ground rent (*see page 26*).

17th-century farmhouse, Troutbeck

Details and decoration

62

Hartsop farmhouse with spinning gallery

Art and Literature

Literature

Lakeland literature is enlivened by the writings of **Dorothy** and **William Wordsworth**, brother and sister, who were born at Cockermouth, sojourned for a while in the South and returned to live in the Lake District, at Dove Cottage, Grasmere, in 1799. Dorothy's prose work is best seen in her *Journal*. Apart from his immense output of verse, William wrote a perceptive guide book to the area. Wordsworth and his friends, including **Samuel Taylor Coleridge**, **Robert Southey** and **Thomas De Quincey**, became known as the Lake Poets. Southey, who settled for a while in Keswick, was appointed Poet Laureate in 1813.

The Lake District was home for an appreciable period to **John Ruskin** (at Brantwood, above Coniston Water), **Hugh Walpole** (at Brackenburn, near Grange-in-Borrowdale), **Arthur Ransome** (who drew partly on memories of childhood holidays at Nibthwaite, by Coniston Water for his *Swallows and Amazons* and many other books), and **Beatrix Potter** (Sawrey, near Hawkshead).

Arthur Ransome remembered in Kendal

Beatrix Potter

A stylish writer in prose and verse who drew much of his creative strength from contemplation of the basic rocks of the Lake District and life in his native, industrialised Millom, was **Norman Nicholson**. Lakeland novels were produced by **Graham Sutton**, who lived near Keswick. In his classic *Fell Days*, he reproduced his hilarious short story, 'The Man Who Broke the Needle', a reference to the celebrated 'stack' on the flanks of Great Gable. A climber who thought he had broken it by dislodging the piece at the top was relieved to find he was dreaming while languishing in his dentist's chair. The needle had broken.

Art

To list the artists who have been inspired by the Lake District would be to risk writer's cramp. They include the incomparable **J.M.W. Turner**, who on a tour in 1797, with the Romantic Age in full swing, produced *Morning amongst the Coniston Fells*, which is at the Tate Gallery. Engravings and drawings in vast numbers were produced commercially by **William Green**, who settled in Ambleside a few years later. **John Constable**, on a single visit (in 1806) made lots of sketches and water-colours but later confessed he had found the mountains oppressive.

Of modern artists, **Delmar Banner** had a genius for presenting Lakeland fells wrapped in cloud. A special tribute should be paid to the Cooper family. At the Heaton Cooper Studio in Grasmere is a permanent exhibition of water-colours and a large collection of colour reproductions of the Lake District by **W. Heaton Cooper** (1903–95) and his father, **A. Heaton Cooper** (1863–1929).

The Warcop Rushbearing

Festivals and Folklore

For centuries, the Lake District proper was a secluded, little-known corner of England, too close to the Scottish border for comfort, and keeping largely to itself. Sheep farming was a primary activity, and entertainment was homespun. Lakelanders developed a love of **sport**, **song** and **dance** (to the strains of fiddle or accordion). Vital events such as the **shepherd's meet**, when stray sheep from the 'gathering' were returned to their rightful owners, saw an explosion of local feeling in **fox-hunting** and, later, **hound-trailing**. At the end of the day, the Cumbrian dalesman resorted to hard drinking, lusty singing, and much eating of **tatie pot** (a local type of stew).

Cumberland and Westmorland wrestling, which is claimed to be the type used when Jacob wrestled with the Angel, demands brains as well as brawn and began with school lads 'takking 'od' (taking hold) on a village green. Such wrestling became respectable when it was to be seen at the **Grasmere Sports**, held in August, which was patronised by Lord Lonsdale from Lowther Park. Among the more bizarre forms of expression which once was in vogue and now survives at **Egremont** was **gurning** (pulling the funniest face) through a **braffin** (horse-collar). A novel event in Wasdale, attended by much drinking and hilarity, is a competition to find **t'biggest liar**, thus keeping alive a tradition dating back to Will Ritson, of **Wasdale Head**, a teller of outrageous tales.

The church has conserved much of the local culture. The **Rushbearing** dates back to the days when churches had earthen floors and on a specified day freshly-cut rushes were spread on the ground. Rushbearings at Ambleside (first Saturday in July) and Grasmere (Saturday nearest 5 August) are processional, attracting large crowds.

Rushbearing mural in Ambleside Church

Festivals calendar

Tourist Information has precise dates (*see page 75*).

May

Cartmel Races (late spring Bank Holiday, Saturday and Monday), steeplechasing. Mary Wakefield Music Festival at Kendal. Fell Pony Stallion Show at Dalemain.

June

Appleby Horse Fair, Gallows Hill near Appleby, one of the country's largest gatherings of gypsy folk, some with vardos (horse-drawn caravans). Warcop Rushbearing, in the Eden Valley between Brough and Appleby; military band; procession of children, boys with rush crosses, girls with floral headdresses. Service in church.

Rush cross

July

Ambleside Rushbearing (first Saturday), procession to church, singing of a special Rushbearing hymn. Musgrave Rushbearing. Penrith Agricultural Show. Keswick Convention, large Christian gathering, spread over two weeks. Cumberland County Show, Carlisle. Cumbria Steam Gathering at Flookburgh, near Grange-over-Sands. Lakeland Rose Show, Kendal (second weekend).

August

Ambleside Sports (Thursday before first Monday). Grasmere Rushbearing (Saturday nearest the 5th). Ambleside Great Summer Flower Show and Craft Fair. Lowther Horse Driving Trials and Country Fair, Lowther Castle, near Penrith. Vale of Rydal Sheepdog Trials, near Ambleside (second Thursday after the first Monday). Grasmere Sports. Kendal Gathering (17-day festival). Keswick Show and Sheepdog Competition. Threlkeld Sheepdog Trials (third Wednesday after first Monday). Cartmel Races, Bank Holiday (Saturday and Monday).

September

Kirkby Lonsdale Victorian Fair. Hawkshead Show (first Tuesday). Westmorland County Show, Kendal (second Thursday). Borrowdale Shepherds Meet and Show. Cartmel Show (early). Loweswater and Brackenthwaite Show (third Thursday). Egremont Crab Fair and Sports (third Saturday). Eskdale Show, Boot. Ulverston Lantern Procession (mid-month).

A shepherd and his flock

October

Windermere Marathon (last Sunday). Wasdale Show, Wasdale Head (second Saturday).

November

Biggest liar in the world competition, Wasdale.

Food and Drink

Traditionally, it was **poddish** (porridge) for breakfast. This was served so thick that a mouse might walk dry-shod across it. Working on the principle that *it's your stomach 'at 'ods your back up*, the Lakeland-born dined heartily on **tatie pot**, a glorious mixture of savoury items and potatoes, frequently served as a supper during some hectic round of dancing. The lile **Herdwick**, as the native sheep was called, might have poor quality wool but its meat was regarded as mutton fit for a king. The Cumberland-style **sausage** is produced in a large herby coil, and it traditionally has good lumps of fat within to help with the cooking. Variations on the theme are smoked sausages made of wild boar and venison. Cumberland cured gammon steak is another delicacy to ask about.

Cumberland sausage

Curiously, when **Windermere char** (deepwater fish) are offered for sale in the Bowness area, it is the butcher, not the fishmonger, who stocks it. And usually the available char are rapidly bought up by emissaries from the big hotels. At Grasmere, the smell of fresh gingerbread flavours the air and leads visitors to the **Gingerbread Shop** (9am–5.45pm weekdays, 12.30–5.30pm Sunday). September is the time to tour the Lyth Valley, southeast of Bowness, for **damsons**. A roadside stall usually has a good supply, though in some years fruit is scarce. Jennings Brewery at Cockermouth has been brewing **ale** since 1828 and has daily tours of their Castle Brewery from March to October, tel: (01900) 823214. Visitors see the processes involved and are invited to sample the end result.

Locally-caught trout

67

Restaurant and tearoom selection

The following is a selection of recommended restaurants in the main centres of the Lake District. Tearooms are included because of the long association with local tourism. They are listed according to three categories:

£££ = expensive; ££ = moderate; £ = inexpensive.

The Glass House Restaurant

Ambleside
The Glass House Cafe Restaurant (£), tel. (015394) 32137. A 16th-century woollen mill, situated behind the famous Bridge House. Mediterranean and modern British food for the discriminating. Daytime offerings include fresh scones, apple cake and clotted cream. **Stampers Restaurant** (££), Church Street (cellar restaurant in the Old Stamp House), tel: (015394) 32775. Local fresh produce, including vegetarian dishes. Evening. **Rothay Garth Hotel and Loughrigg Restaurant** (££), Rothay Road, Freephone O500 657865. Elegant and award-winning. **Rothay Manor** (£££), Rothay Bridge. Luxury hotel and highly commended restaurant. tel: (015394) 33605.

Appleby

The Castle (£). Historic range of buildings, rare breeds of animals and birds – and a Café and Tea Rooms. March to October, daily 10am–5pm.

Bowness

The Porthole

The Porthole (££), tel: (015394) 42793. Converted 17th-century cottage with dining downstairs or at front of restaurant. Italian, French and English cuisine, with vegetarian dishes available. Bar, Italian patio and balcony upstairs. World of Beatrix Potter attraction includes the **Tailor of Gloucester's Tea Room** (£).

Cartmel

Cavendish Arms Hotel (££), tel: (015395) 36240. An old coaching inn (16th-century) with its own brewery and high reputation for its catering.

Eskdale

The King's Arms in Cartmel

The Woolpack Inn (£), tel: (019467) 23230. Well-known hostelry in western Lake District. Good food with a selection of real ale.

Grange-in-Borrowdale

The Borrowdale Gates Country House Hotel (££), tel: (017687) 77204. Fine food each evening cooked by the chef-patron. Light lunches and afternoon teas in the lounges.

Grasmere

Dove Cottage Tearoom (£). Near the famous Grasmere home of William Wordsworth. The tearoom is open throughout the day, with a special family rate.

Grizedale

Grizedale Lodge Hotel and Restaurant in the Forest (££), tel: (015394) 36532. In the heart of Grizedale Forest, approached from near Hawkshead. Food served under personal supervision of proprietors. Useful for those attending events at the nearby Theatre in the Forest.

Kendal

The Café Restaurant (£), The Brewery Art Centre, tel: (01539) 725133. Lunch may be taken on garden patio. In the evening, the speciality items are bistro-style dishes, 'naughty puds' and cinema suppers (two-course meal plus cinema ticket). **Abbot Art Gallery** (£), near the Church. Free parking for visitors. Lunch and refreshments in the coffee shop. **The Barn Shop and Tearoom** (££), Low Sizergh Farm, beside the Kendal by-pass, tel: (01539) 560426. 17th-century stone barn, with farm shop (selling Cumbrian produce) and rustic tearoom overlooking the milking parlour, where cows are milked at about 3.30pm daily.

Keswick
The Rembrandt Restaurant (£), Station Street, tel: (017687) 72008. Traditional food, including steak and kidney pie. Home-made sweets. **Bryson's Bakery and Tea Rooms** (£), Main Street, tel: (017687) 72257. Wide range of meals from breakfast to cream teas. Open seven days during the season. **Lairbeck Hotel** (££), Vicarage Hill, tel: (017687) 73373. Fresh food, carefully prepared. **Mirehouse** (£), 3½ miles north of Keswick on A591. Family home for three centuries. Old Sawmill Tearoom noted for its generous local-style home cooking.

Far Sawrey, Hawkshead
The Sawrey Hotel (££), tel: (015394) 43425. Licensed country inn in Beatrix Potter country. Wide choice on a menu that is changed daily.

The Queen's Head in Hawkshead

Newby Bridge
Swan Hotel (££), tel: (015395) 31681. Beside the Leven, the overflow of Windermere. Tithe Barn restaurant or the less formal Mailcoach. Licensed bars.

69

Skelwith Bridge
Kirkstone Galleries (£). Beside the Ambleside-Coniston Road at the junction to Great Langdale. A café serving home-made cakes. Open through the year, 10am–6pm in summer, closing at 5pm in the off-season.

Kirkstone Pass Inn

Thirlspot, near Keswick
The King's Head Hotel (££), tel: freephone 0500 600725. Former 17th-century coaching inn beside Keswick–Grasmere road near the foot of Helvellyn. Traditional English fare, real ales.

Ullswater
Dalemain (£), historic house, home of Hazells for 300 years, on the A592, 3 miles from Junction 40 on the M6. Bar lunches and home-made teas available in a medieval hall. Open 11.15am–5pm except Friday and Saturday.

Windermere
Miller Howe (£££), Rayrigg Road, tel: (015394) 42536. John Tovey's well-known restaurant, for gourmets who like immaculate service. **Lakeland Plastics** (£), near the railway station. Catering by John Tovey, the area having been extended. **Brockhole Visitor Centre** (£), National Park between Windermere and Ambleside. Excellent restaurant and tea rooms. Open April to October.

Active Holidays

Variations on the 'activity' theme in an area of mountains, crags and lakes are limitless. The holiday brochure published by the Tourist Board mentions a selection at random to indicate the scope – 'walking and weaving, pony trekking and painting, quilting or canoeing'. Also available are paragliding, golfing, mountain biking, trekking, walking and angling.

Come prepared for all weathers

Walking

The most common form of recreation in the Lake District is walking, and the best-known handbooks for walkers are the Pictorial Guides of Alfred Wainwright. The original edition is now somewhat out of date but is being revised. The shelves of Lake District bookshops are crammed with guide books, most of which describe walking circular routes. The Ordnance Survey maps are the most detailed. The Lake District National Park organises walks for visitors, details being given in their free newspaper, which is available at any Information Centre. The Cumbria Tourist Board issues a booklet entitled *Short Walks Good for Families*.

A good short walk (about 2½ hours) is round **Buttermere**, one of the quieter lakes, starting at a car park in the village. The route is suitable for visitors in wheelchairs. Somewhat longer is the circumnavigation of **Grasmere** and **Rydal**, beginning at one of the car parks of Grasmere and walking on a well-beaten path to the west of the lakes, one stretch of the way being the celebrated **Loughrigg Terrace**. Return to Grasmere on a hillside path which begins near Rydal Mount (*see page 38*).

The Langdale Valley

Among the popular but more exacting hill walks of the Lake District is a circuit taking in the **Langdale Pikes**, beginning and ending at the Dungeon Ghyll car park at the head of Great Langdale. In the east of the region, the summit of **Helvellyn** can be approached from either Thirlmere or Ullswater, a possible route from the latter being up the magnificent Striding Edge. In Central Lakeland, **Great Gable** can be ascended from Honister Pass, Styhead Tarn from the head of Borrowdale or Wasdale Head. Wasdale Head is the most popular departure point for those wishing to conquer **Scafell Pike**. The southern fells are dominated by **Coniston Old Man** and **Skiddaw** looms over to the north. Skiddaw's summit is an easy hike from Millbeck, to the north of Keswick.

Climbing

Climbing is not a sport that can be undertaken casually. Many young people learn the techniques through Outward Bound or Field Centres. Wasdale is a favourite of many

Sailing on Windemere

an experienced climber. Langdale and Coniston rock is durable and popular. Climbers might be seen on crags near the Jaws of Borrowdale, and there are some nursery pitches not far from the Bowder Stone.

Cycling and pony trekking

A long slog up the Wrynose **71**

There has been a rapid increase in the number of mountain bikers using the Lake District. It is possible to hire a mountain bike (all-terrain bicycle or ATB) in Ambleside, Kendal, Keswick and Windermere. The Cumbria Cycle Way of 280 miles (450km) is a circular, waymarked route for which quiet country roads were chosen. The marks of cycle tyres are now seen near the imprint of walking boots and the shoes of the stocky pony used for trekking. Some of the ponies are of the fell breed, which has ranged the Lake District fells for centuries.

Water and other sports

Canoeing course

Watersports are well-catered for around Windermere, where power boats (and therefore water-skiing) are still allowed. On Windermere there are a few zones where speed is restricted. There is a speed limit of 10mph (16kph) on Derwentwater and Coniston Water. On other lakes, powerboats are not permitted to operate. Unusual ways of tuning up the body as well as the mind include gorge-scrambling, aquasailing and (at Flookburgh) parachuting. There are sports centres at Kendal, Keswick and Cockermouth. Golf flourishes on 15 good-sized courses, and day tickets are available.

Fishing

Anglers need a North West Water Authority rod licence (inquire at any tackle shop) plus a fishing permit. Look out at an information centre for the *Westmorland Gazette* guide to angling in the district.

Getting There

Opposite: making for the summit

By plane

Overseas visitors find Manchester Airport most convenient for Cumbria. Manchester is adjacent to the M6, which runs along the eastern fringe of the Lake District.

By road

Vintage arrival

The Lake District is about five hours from London by road, using the motorway system. The M6 gives quick access to the Lake District, with points of exit at Lancaster, Kendal by-pass, Shap and Penrith. By road from Dover to Windermere is 353 miles (570km); from the North Sea ferry at Hull to Windermere is 139 miles (224km).

By train

Inter-City services from London to Oxenholme (connecting with a local service to Windermere) take 3 hours. Inter-City trains from Edinburgh to Carlisle take 1½ hours, a little longer to Penrith. The Leeds–Settle–Carlisle railway is served by Sprinter diesel units. A rail service on the scenic Cumbrian Coast route connects Lancaster, Barrow-in-Furness, Whitehaven and Carlisle. Details from any railway station or tel: (0171) 387 7070.

73

Grange-over-Sands station

Getting Around

For details of bus and rail services throughout Cumbria, contact Travel Link, tel: (01228) 812812, or consult the nearest Tourist Information Centre (*see page 75*).

By train

The 72-mile Settle–Carlisle line is of high scenic interest, travelling through the north–south valleys of Ribble and Eden between the Lakeland fells and the Pennines with high country in between that features huge viaducts and long tunnels. Equally impressive is the system which takes in the Cumbrian Coast, from Lancaster or Barrow-in-Furness to Carlisle. Starting from Lancaster allows a return from Carlisle to Lancaster by Inter-City over Shap Fell and through the Lune Gorge.

Ravenglass and Eskdale Railway

Ravenglass and Eskdale Railway, nicknamed Ratty, is England's oldest narrow-gauge steam railway. It operates over 7 miles (11km) of track through arresting scenery. For more information, tel: (01229) 717171.

Lakeside & Haverthwaite Railway connects at Lakeside, Windermere, with a 'steamer' voyage to Bowness and Waterhead. At Haverthwaite, beside the A590, is a car park, refreshment room, shop and display of locomotives. For more information, tel: (015395) 31594.

By car

Congestion in Bowness

The car is the handiest form of transport in the Lakes, but at peak times it causes acute congestion, and there are calls from some preservation groups for car controls in the Park. Finding parking may be difficult at the height of the season. At the head of Kentmere, for example, lots of cones are in place, and parking near the church has been restricted. A local field is open, and a charge is made at the busiest times. Most car parks now have pay-and-display facilities. The machines do not give change, so carry a variety of coins. Or, in the case of National Park car parks, inquire about season tickets. Most of the main centres, such as Windermere and Ambleside, have one-way traffic systems in operation. This also applies to the main area of the car parks at Bowness Bay.

By bus

The main bus companies are Ribble and CMS Cumberland. CMS Cumberland operates a bus into Borrowdale.

By boat

Hundreds of boats are to be seen on Windermere at the height of the season. Windermere Lake Cruises, operating from Lakeside, mountains a year-round service using traditional 'steamers', *Swan*, *Swift*, *Teal* and *Tern*, from Ambleside, Bowness and Lakeside, with a summer connection with the Lakeside & Haverthwaite Steam Railway and the National Park Visitor Centre at Brockhole. For information, contact the Windermere Iron Steamboat Company, Lakeside, tel: (015395) 31188. All-weather motor cruisers operate trips from Bowness Bay.

On Derwentwater, near Keswick, some motor launches operate to timetable, maintaining a valuable transport link with piers around the lake. The National Trust steam yacht *Gondola*, first launched in 1859, sails to a timetable on Coniston Water, tel: (015394) 41288.

The Gondola experience

Ullswater Steamers (*MV Raven* and *MV Lady of the Lake*) runs three daily services, April to October, between Glenridding, Howtown and Pooley Bridge and 1-hour cruises from Glenridding. Refreshments and bars on board. Inquiries at Glenridding Pier, tel: (017684) 82229.

In a guided party

Mountain Goat Tours, Victoria Street, Windermere, tel: (015394) 45161. Mini-coaches with panoramic windows.
Lakeland Safari, 23 Fisherbeck Park, Ambleside, tel: (015394) 33904. Various tours in six-seater vehicles.
Lakes Supertours, 1 High Street, Windermere, tel: (015394) 88133. Small informal groups in mini-coaches. Tours are also arranged by Browns of Ambleside, a long-established firm.

Facts for the Visitor

Tourist Information Centres

The Cumbria Tourist Board has its headquarters at Ashleigh, Holly Road, Windermere, LA23 2AQ, tel: (015394) 44444, fax: (015394) 44041.

The following are centres at which verbal and printed information is available. An asterisk (*) represents centres that are open throughout the year.

*Ambleside, The Old Courthouse, Church Street, tel: (015394) 32582; ***Appleby-in-Westmorland**, Moot Hall, Boroughgate, tel: (017683) 51177; ***Barrow-in-Furness**, Forum 28, Duke Street, tel: (01229) 870156; **Bowness-on-Windermere**, Glebe Road, Bowness Bay, tel: (015394) 42895; ***Cockermouth**, The Town Hall, tel: (01900) 822634; **Coniston**, Ruskin Avenue, tel: (015394) 41533; ***Grange-over-Sands**, Victoria Hall, Main Street, tel: (015395) 34026; **Grasmere**, Red Bank Road, tel: (015394) 35245; **Hawkshead**, Main Car Park, tel: (015394) 36525; ***Kendal**, Town Hall, Highgate, tel: (01539) 725758; ***Keswick**, Moot Hall, Market Square, tel: (017687) 72645; ***Kirkby Lonsdale**, 24 Main Street, tel: (015242) 71437; ***Maryport**, Maryport Maritime Museum, 1 Senhouse Street, tel: (01900) 813738; ***Penrith**, Penrith Museum, Middlegate, tel: (01768) 867466; **Pooley Bridge**, The Square, tel: (017684) 86530; **Ullswater**, Main Car Park, Glenridding, tel: (017684) 82414; ***Ulverston**, Coronation Hall, County Square, tel: (01229) 587120; **Waterhead**, Car Park, Ambleside, tel: (015394) 32729; ***Whitehaven**, Market Hall, Market Place, tel: (01946) 695678; ***Windermere**, Victoria Street, tel: (015394) 46499.

Images of Bowness Pier

Ambleside

Peter Rabbit

Wordsworth House plaque

IN THIS HOUSE WAS BORN
ON APRIL 7TH 1770
WILLIAM WORDSWORTH,
POET LAUREATE.
HE DIED AT RYDAL MOUNT, GRASMERE
APRIL 23RD 1850.
INTERRED IN GRASMERE CHURCHYARD.
DOROTHY HIS SISTER 1771-1855

National Trust

Information Centres

Bridge House, **Ambleside**; Lakeside, **Keswick**; The Square, **Hawkshead**; Wordsworth House, **Cockermouth**; Fell Foot Country Park, **Newby Bridge**. For information, tel: (015395) 31273 or (015394) 35599

Principal Attractions

Beatrix Potter Gallery, Hawkshead, tel: (015394) 36355. Exhibition, changed annually, of original illustrations from the famous children's stories. Gallery in office of Beatrix's husband, who was a solicitor.

    Beatrix Potter's Lake District, Keswick, tel: (017687) 75173. Slide and video presentations relating to Beatrix's conservation work. She bequeathed a considerable amount of property and land to the National Trust.

    Wordsworth House, Cockermouth, tel: (01900) 824805. A Georgian town house, the birthplace of William Wordsworth in 1770. Seven rooms are furnished in 18th-century style.

    Fell Foot Park and Garden, Newby Bridge, tel: (015395) 31273. Attractive venue for a day trip near the outflow of Windermere. Rhododendrons and daffodils. Rowing boats for hire.

    Townend, Troutbeck (Windermere), tel: (015394) 32628. Early 17th-century farmhouse containing carved woodwork and other objects kept over several centuries by the Brownes, a yeoman family.

Lake District National Park

Lake District National Park Authority, Kendal, tel: 01539 72455. National Park Visitor Centre, Brockhole, tel: (015394) 46601. A stylish house in large grounds just north of Windermere has exhibitions, a shop, café, adventure playground, gardens, a wildflower meadow with hundreds of plant species, a walk along a lakeside path and a memorable view of the Langdale Pikes. There is no admission fee, but a charge is made for car parking.

Maps

Four Ordnance Survey maps in the Outdoor Leisure series (maps 4–7) at a scale of 1:25,000 (2½ inches to 1 mile or 4cm to 1km) cover the Lake District, taking over from the OS Pathfinder maps, which are still available for the peripheral areas. The maps are stocked by most good bookshops and stationers. They are recommended because they have great clarity and show field boundaries. Footpaths are clearly marked by hatched green lines. For cyclists, the Cumbria Tourist Board has a Touring Map available by post for £2 including postage from Ashleigh, Holly Road, Windermere, Cumbria, LA23 2AQ.

Gull over Windermere

Lake District for Children

Grizedale sculpture playground

Facilities range from theme attractions, such as those associated with **Beatrix Potter**, to adventurous activity like **camping** and **canoeing**, as written about so evocatively by Arthur Ransome in *Swallows and Amazons* (expert tuition is available in most areas). As indicated, **Brockhole Visitor Centre** has special arrangements for children, with hands-on possibilities. An adventure playground is varied and imaginative. Older children may like to try their hand at **drystone walling**.

77

Lowther Leisure and Wildlife Park, close to the A6, south of Penrith, is open from March to September. On 150 acres (61 hectares) are varied attractions. An hour-long circus show and miniature railway are appealing to children. There is also an adventure playground. In the park are red deer, descendants of those which ranged the Lakeland fells centuries ago. Also at Lowther, with a separate entrance near the village, is the **Lakeland Bird of Prey Centre**. Birds are flown daily. Visitors who wander around see hawks, eagles and owls at close quarters.

Keswick has for long been a famous place for pencil-making. How the industry came into existence, and how pencils are made, can be seen at the **Pencil Museum** adjacent to the works. Years ago, graphite mined at the head of Borrowdale was used for pencil-making. Young people who enjoy visiting remoter country might be taken to the head of Borrowdale, where the evidence of mining is still to be seen on the fellside. (Stay above ground!)

Remoter country

Pony trekking is an adventurous way of seeing the country. The ponies follow the green tracks on which, years ago, packhorse trains operated, moving goods from one settlement to another and carrying wool into Kendal for processing. Another form of transport popular with children is the **Ravenglass and Eskdale Railway**.

Accommodation

Lake District accommodation is listed in a free guide available from Information Centres or the Cumbria Tourist Board (*see page 75*). The following recommendations are open all year unless otherwise stated. The basic cost for one person sharing a twin/double room is shown by:

£££ over £60; ££ £30–60; £ under £30

Wateredge Hotel

Ambleside

Borrans Park Hotel (££), tel: (015394) 33454. Home cooking, log fires, four-poster beds. **Waterhead Hotel** (££), Lake Road, tel: (015394) 32566. On Windermere lake; modernised, good food. **Wateredge Hotel** (££), Waterhead Bay, tel: (015394) 32332. Family-run hotel with pleasant gardens down to the lake. **Brantfell** (£), Rothay Road, tel: (015394) 32239. Victorian house with views; traditional/vegetarian food. **Fisherbeck Farm House** (£), Old Lake Road, tel: (015394) 32523. Quiet with great breakfasts; March to November.

78

Greenbank

Borrowdale

Hazel Bank (££), Rosthwaite, tel: (017687) 77248. Highly commended; non-smoking; April to November. **Greenbank** (£££), tel: (017687) 77215. **Derwent House** (£), Grange, tel: (017687) 77658. Victorian guest house; log fires and limited smoking. **Seatoller House** (£), near dale head, tel: (017687) 77218. Informal; good food.

Coniston

Beech Tree (£), tel: (015394) 41717. Former vicarage. February–December. **Sun Hotel** (£), tel: (015394) 41248. 16th-century inn. **Yewdale Hotel** (£), Yewdale Road, tel: (015394) 41280. Restaurant; January–December.

Ennerdale Bridge

Shepherd's Arms Hotel (£), tel: (01946) 861249. Traditional village inn; serves salmon and game.

Eskdale

The Bower House Inn (££), Holmrook, tel: (019467) 23244. Old inn with log fire and good food. **The Brook House Hotel** (£), Boot, tel: (019467) 23288. Victorian hotel by Ravenglass-Eskdale Railway; real ale.

Grasmere

Ash Cottage (££), Red Lion Square, tel: (015394) 35224. February–December. **Titteringales Guest House** (£), Pye Lane, tel: (015394) 35439. Good views; parking. **Lake View Country House** (£), Lake View Drive, tel: (015394) 35384. Overlooking Grasmere lake. February–December.

Grange-over-Sands and Cartmel
Aynsome Manor Hotel (££), Vale of Cartmel, tel: (015395) 36653. 16th-century manor. February–December. **Greenacres Guest House** (£), Lindale, tel: 015395 34578. 19th-century cottage in pleasant village.

Hawkshead
Silverholme (££), Graythwaite, tel: (015395) 31332. Small Georgian mansion on west Lake Windermere. **Sun Inn** (£), Main Street, tel: (015394) 36236. 17th-century inn. **Garth Country House** (£), Near Sawrey, tel: (015-394) 36373. By Esthwaite Water; February–November.

Kendal District
Jolly Anglers' Inn (£), Burneside, tel: (01539) 732552. Free fishing; attached cottages. **Low Jock Star** (£), Selside, tel: (01539) 823259. Secluded riverside setting.

Low Jock Scar Guesthouse

Keswick District
Stakis Ladore Swiss (£££), Ladore Falls, tel: (017687) 77285). Luxury hotel with excellent facilities. **Aaron Lodge** (£), Stationmaster's house, tel: (017687) 72399. 5 minutes from town centre. **The Anchorage** (£), Ambleside Road, tel: (017687) 72813. Near lake and park. Good views; non-smoking; February–November. **The Mill** (££), Mungrisdale, tel: (017687) 79659. Former mill cottage. Good food. **The Cottage in the Wood** (£), Whinlatter Pass, tel: (017687) 78409. Former coaching house.

Langdales
New Dungeon Ghyll Hotel (££), Great Langdale, tel: (015394) 37213. In 6 acres of fellside. **Long House** (£), Great Langdale, tel: (015394) 37222. 17th-century cottage. **Three Shires Inn** (££), Little Langdale, tel: (015394) 37215. 19th-century inn.

Ullswater District
Barco House (£), in Patterdale, tel: (017684) 82474. Near lake. **Waterside House** (£), Watermillock, tel: (017684) 86038. 18th-century house on lakeshore. **Park House Farm** (£), Dalemain, tel: (017684) 86212. 18th-century farmhouse by Dalemain House. April–October. **Sharrow Bay** (£££), tel: 017684 86301. Luxury hotel in Italianate style; set in formal gardens overlooking Ullswater.

Windermere and Bowness
Dalegarth Hotel (££), Lake Road, tel: (015394) 45052. Swimming facilities. **Fairfield Hotel** (£), Brantfell Road, Bowness, tel: (015394) 46565. Secluded gardens close to village; January–December. **Firgarth** (£), Ambleside Road, tel: (015394) 46974. By the equestrian centre.

Index